BRING NSCAA COACHING EDUCATION TO YOUR COMMUNITY!

For more information visit **NSCAA.com/request-a-course** or call **816-471-1941**.

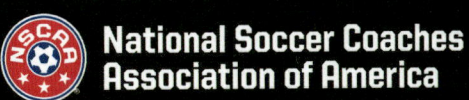

National Soccer Coaches Association of America

COACHING 4V4, 7V7 & 9V9 SMALL SIDED SOCCER – VOLUME 1

EDITED BY
David Newbery - eLearning Coordinator, NSCAA

ACTIVITY CONTRIBUTIONS BY

David Newbery, eLearning Coordinator, NSCAA
Mark Spiegel, Make Your Own Ball Day Founder.
Vince Ganzberg, Education Coordinator, NSCAA.
Ian Mulliner, Massachusetts Youth Soccer.
Ian Barker, NSCAA Director of Coaching Education.

FRONT COVER DESIGN, ACTIVITY ILLUSTRATIONS AND LAYOUT

David Newbery, eLearning Coordinator, NSCAA

REVIEWER

Valerie Brown

PRODUCED BY

Coaching Media Group

NSCAA eLearning

Copyright © 2015 by Coaching Media Group and NSCAA
Published by Coaching Media Group, PO Box 1586 Westerly, RI 02891 and NSCAA, 30 W. Pershing Rd., Suite 350 Kansas City, MO 64108-2463 · Tel: 816-471-1941. All rights reserved. No part of this work may be reproduced or transmitted in any form, for commercial purposes or by any means electronic or mechanical, including photocopying or recording from any information stored in a retrieval system, without permission from the authors.

TABLE OF CONTENTS

iv MANUAL CONTRIBUTORS
5 contributors to the coaching manual.

v INTRODUCTORY LETTER
Welcome letter from NSCAA

vi A NEW DAWN FOR YOUTH SOCCER
Introduction to small sided games written by David Newbery.

5 SOCCER LEARNING PATHWAY DISCUSSION DOCUMENT?
Questions to ask in preparation for implementing small sided games.

6 ABOUT THE NSCAA PLAYER DEVELOPMENT CURRICULUM
Origins of NSCAA 5 Stage of Development Model.

7 COMPETENCY MATRIX
Foundation framework for managing progress between stages of development.

12 LIST OF ACTIVITIES
List of 42 activities and formation diagrams in the manual.

14 INTRODUCTORY ACTIVITIES
6 activities designed by David Newbery.

21 4v4 FORMATION SLIDES
3 different formations with attacking and defending shape.

24 4v4 ACTIVITIES
12 activities designed by Mark Spiegel.

37 7v7 FORMATION SLIDES
3 different formations with attacking and defending shape.

40 7v7 ACTIVITIES
12 activities designed by Vince Ganzberg.

53 9v9 FORMATION SLIDES
3 different formations with attacking and defending shape.

56 9v9 ACTIVITIES
12 activities designed by Ian Mulliner.

MANUAL CONTRIBUTORS

DAVID NEWBERY, EDITOR AND AUTHOR OF INTRODUCTION TO SMALL SIDED GAMES, 4v4, 7v7 and 9v9

eLearning Coordinator, NSCAA

MARK SPIEGEL, AUTHOR OF SMALL SIDED GAMES – 4v4

Make Your Own Ball Day Founder.

VINCE GANZBERG, AUTHOR OF SMALL SIDED GAMES – 7v7

Education Coordinator, NSCAA

IAN MULLINER, AUTHOR OF SMALL SIDED GAMES – 9v9

Technical Director, Massachusetts Youth Soccer.

IAN BARKER, GENERAL CONTRIBUTOR

Director of Coaching Education, NSCAA

INTRODUCTORY LETTER

Dear Coach,

A coaching manual and education course focusing on small sided games has never been so relevant and applicable as it is today.

The short and long term effects of the US Soccer Federation Player Development initiatives are far reaching, impacting all youth clubs and coaches. Arguably the most significant decision in a decade, the youth soccer landscape is changing rapidly for coaches and administrators. In 2015/16 NSCAA offered an eLearning series dedicated to preparing players, teams and clubs to address the tactical, technical and logistical opportunities presented in this new era in youth soccer. Coaches attending the 'NSCAA Small Sided Games Diploma – 4v4, 7v7 and 9v9' are treated to 4 on-demand presentations including 42 training activities to support the new playing formats. This manual was developed to support the eLearning series.

Critically, we will discuss how clubs can establish a new 'learning pathway' and progress players along the player development continuum. We will also address potential formations and philosophies to ensure teams are prepared for the attacking and defending challenges of 4v4, 7v7 and 9v9. Features of this series include:

- 42 training activities expertly illustrated.
- 3 possible formations for each small sided game format - with attacking and defending shape.
- Practical coaching methods a coach can employ to facilitate player learning.
- Attacking and defending principles with 4v4, 7v7 and 9v9.
- Strengths and challenges of different team formations:
  - 4v4 – 0-2-2; 0-1-3; 0-1-2-1 etc.
  - 7v7 – 1-3-2-1; 1-2-1-3; 1-3-1-2 etc.
  - 9v9 – 1-4-3-1; 1-2-3-3; 1-2-4-2 etc.
- Review U.S. Soccer's mandates - age and player grouping, field sizes and equipment.
- Practical steps a club and coach can take to educate parents of the changes and opportunities.

Our eLearning mantra is 'Education. Where you want it. When you want it. How you want it.' To learn more about NSCAA eLearning, visit www.NSCAA.com/eLearning.

NSCAA is committed to delivering convenient coaching education in a variety of methods – methods that reflect different learning styles and interest levels of our members. Our priority is to present vibrant and engaging content in a low cost elearning format to supplement and enhance existing NSCAA courses and events. It is now possible for a coach, at their convenience, to participate in highly informative and tremendously interesting courses and presentations and receive formal recognition/credit for participation. Benefits of eLearning are considerable, both for the individual and NSCAA.

Expect to see many more low cost opportunities in the near future to engage with top professional educators without the need to leave your home, office or local library. Visit www.NSCAA.com/eLearning to view our extensive library of courses and coaching manuals. We hope you enjoy the manual. Please don't hesitate to provide us with feedback relating to the webinars, manual and discussions.

Kind Regards,

David Newbery
eLearning Coordinator, NSCAA
dnewbery@nscaa.com

Ian Barker
Director of Coaching Education, NSCAA
ibarker@nscaa.com

A NEW DAWN FOR YOUTH SOCCER - Written by David Newbery

Prior to Fall season 2015 U.S. Soccer released details of its Player Development Initiatives, designed to improve the youth soccer landscape at the entry levels. By Fall 2017, more than 10,000 youth clubs, and countless leagues and associations across the U.S. are required to adopt these mandates.

The importance, enormity and scope these changes cannot be understated or ignored. U.S. Soccer has provided clubs with a tremendous opportunity to upgrade coaching education and re-define the approach to player development. It is also an opportunity to address what U.S. Soccer sees as deficiencies in the American 'soccer culture' - an overemphasis on winning and results, instead of focusing on individual skill development.

What steps has your club taken to address player and coach development?

Enthusiasm for the mandates by the youth soccer community has been mixed, but the changes are mostly seen as a positive step forward, particularly in professional coaching circles. With that said, there remains many questions regarding implementation and nervousness by youth clubs particularly relating to the potential impact of age group registration moving to the calendar year.

Anecdotal information seems to suggest the majority of leagues, associations and clubs remain in deep deliberation, debating how best to proceed. As is human nature, a disproportionate amount of time and energy is being spent in meetings discussing the challenges a club will endure, in particular the task of effectively communicating such changes to the organization's Membership. Playing on smaller fields than many clubs are used to is certainly a sticking point, but undoubtedly the most vociferous objections are associated with across the board changes to age groupings. Every youth team in America will be affected. In some cases coaches and administrators are plotting to sidestep the system. For example, the widely adopted 'player pass' program enabling Coaching Directors flexibility to move players between teams in an effort to enhance their individual development, is now considered a mechanism to move players 'en masse' to keep teams together.

All tactics and no strategy!

In large part, the Development Initiatives are considered to be logical and follow a well-trodden player development path. However, the principal challenge facing youth soccer in US is not the efficacy of the plan, but the inadequate processes and systems to execute the plan. Who or what has responsibility and the authority to ensure successful implementation of these changes - to reach over 10,000 youth clubs scattered over 3.79 million square miles within 18 months? U.S. Soccer, US Youth Soccer, State Associations, US Club Soccer, AYSO, SAY, independent league organizers?

Responsibility to achieve success has been unmistakably passed to the youth clubs. Similar to other decentralized models such as school education, nursing, policing, and municipal government, national and regional governance is limited, with preference given to local management and decision making. To this end there is no single National or State level entity with the resources or operational capability to ensure consistent adoption in all communities. Consequently, the success of the Development Initiatives, thought necessary by U.S. Soccer to address a prevailing 'winning culture,'

This article first appeared in NSCAA Soccer Journal, Jan/Feb 2016

are now the responsibility of clubs faulted for the status of the youth game in the first place. Feedback from several state associations suggest education interventions are being planned and executed to support members. An area receiving particular emphasis is coaching education, the mandates perceived as an ideal catalyst to engage members and encourage participation in more frequent training.

Benefits for Coaching

The benefits for coaches of the Small Sided Games mandates should not be understated. Inconsistent game formats make the job of coaching significantly more challenging and planning for player development with a high degree of certainty ineffective. Clubs can now plan coaching education to meet the challenges and opportunities facing coaches as they navigate their players and teams along the progressive pathway towards 11v11 games. Equally, coaches can develop their philosophies, coaching plans and content to support a long term development approach. For example, a coach that believes in building play from the goalkeeper through the defensive, midfield and attacking lines of the team can now establish a teaching blueprint for 4v4, 7v7, 9v9 and 11v11. Movement to national mandated playing formats should be applauded by Coaches, Parents and Administrators.

A Rationale for Small Sided Games – Player Benefits

In the last decade numerous research studies in soccer and other sports have been conducted to determine if performance, emotional and cognitive benefits exist for young players participating in small sided games. Different playing formats have been tested with the same age groups to determine which format is best. The evidence pointing to the benefits of small sided games is conclusive as evidenced in the list below. What is less indisputable is what the best format for a particular age group is.

One can argue that developmental readiness is far more important than the age of the player, particularly considering developmental differences - plus or minus 2 years of chronological age have been reported for children of the same age. One does not however need to conduct a formal research project to instantly recognize opportunities small sided games offer our young players. It is anticipated a parent or coach observing an appropriate small sided game format see many of the benefits listed:

1. Fewer players on the field increases the likelihood of individuals contacting the ball.
2. Fewer players increase the size of the available space and consequently the game encourages players to be more physically active as they have to cover more ground.
3. Players are more readily involved in attacking and defending situations.
4. At the youngest age groups where chasing after the ball is commonplace, there are less players chasing after the player with the ball.
5. Fewer decisions to make in a less complicated and easier to understand environment.
6. A gradual transition in player numbers creates a clear learning pathway for coaches to plan player development opportunities commensurate with the child's physical, emotional and cognitive readiness.
7. Players report to having more fun in contrast to playing games with more players.
8. Goal scoring opportunities are generally more frequent and more players are in a position to score.
9. Better utilization of available field space results in more players playing and less watching.
10. The number of 'lines of interaction' are limited. These are the potential number of passing options for the player on the ball. Each time a player is removed from the field, the decision making difficulty of the game environment decreases.

Learning Pathway

A soccer learning pathway is defined as the ideal sequence of learning experiences to reach a level of competence – in this case to play 11v11. The list of learning experiences is numerous and includes: small sided games, pick-up games, training, self-directed training time, supplemental training (such as speed and agility) and cross training with other sports. Interestingly, NSCAA Club Standards Project's research with over 175 youth clubs in USA and Canada has revealed very few organizations have a clearly defined learning pathway. Routinely, clubs offer a variety of learning experiences that are disconnected and rarely build towards an end goal or objective. If your organization does not have a well-defined learning pathway or one that has been updated to address new small sided game formats, now is an excellent time to discuss, debate and create a Learning Pathway covering the entire youth soccer experience. Engaging all key constituent groups contributing to programming for infants, pre-adolescent, adolescents and young adults through the ages of 18 is critically important. This is no small task but is essential for organizations seeking to raise coaching and playing standards. To support clubs we have created a 'Soccer Learning Pathway Discussion Document' with 14 questions to assist clubs in the planning process on page 5.

Player Development Continuum

One of the inevitable challenges of designing a Learning Pathway is accounting for development variability of children from the same age group. One must ask the question – Will all or only some of the learners have the physical, mental and emotional readiness to benefit fully from the experience? The diagram below illustrates a rudimentary overview of the youth soccer experience featuring the Learning Pathway, Continuum of Player Development and Competencies.

Individuals having had opportunities to coach infant and pre-pubescent players U12 and younger will attest to observing noticeable development differences between age groups, within age groups and between genders. Furthermore, during the formative years of participation it is common to see individual performance levels fluctuate dramatically during relatively short periods in the same season. With this in mind, it is possible for the learning pathway and the performance capabilities of players to be out of synch. Failure to recognize and plan for this eventuality may lead to players frustrated or bored by experiences not meeting their level of competence or commitment, and potentially leading to dropout from the sport.

Transitioning Players Along the Continuum

To further illustrate this point, let's consider the transition from 4v4 to 7v7 – 2 'events' along the learning pathway. I have previously discussed that smaller player numbers increase the likelihood of touches of the ball, greater engagement of players and improved probabilities of scoring etc. Correspondingly, each time a player is added to the field the degree of complexity increases. In fact, the potential number of passing options for the player on the ball jumps dramatically from 4v4 – 12 lines of interaction to 7v7 – 42 lines of interaction. To be precise the game becomes 300% more challenging for an 8 year old (U9) playing 7v7, than for a 7 year old (U8) playing 4v4.

It is incumbent on the leadership of youth clubs to

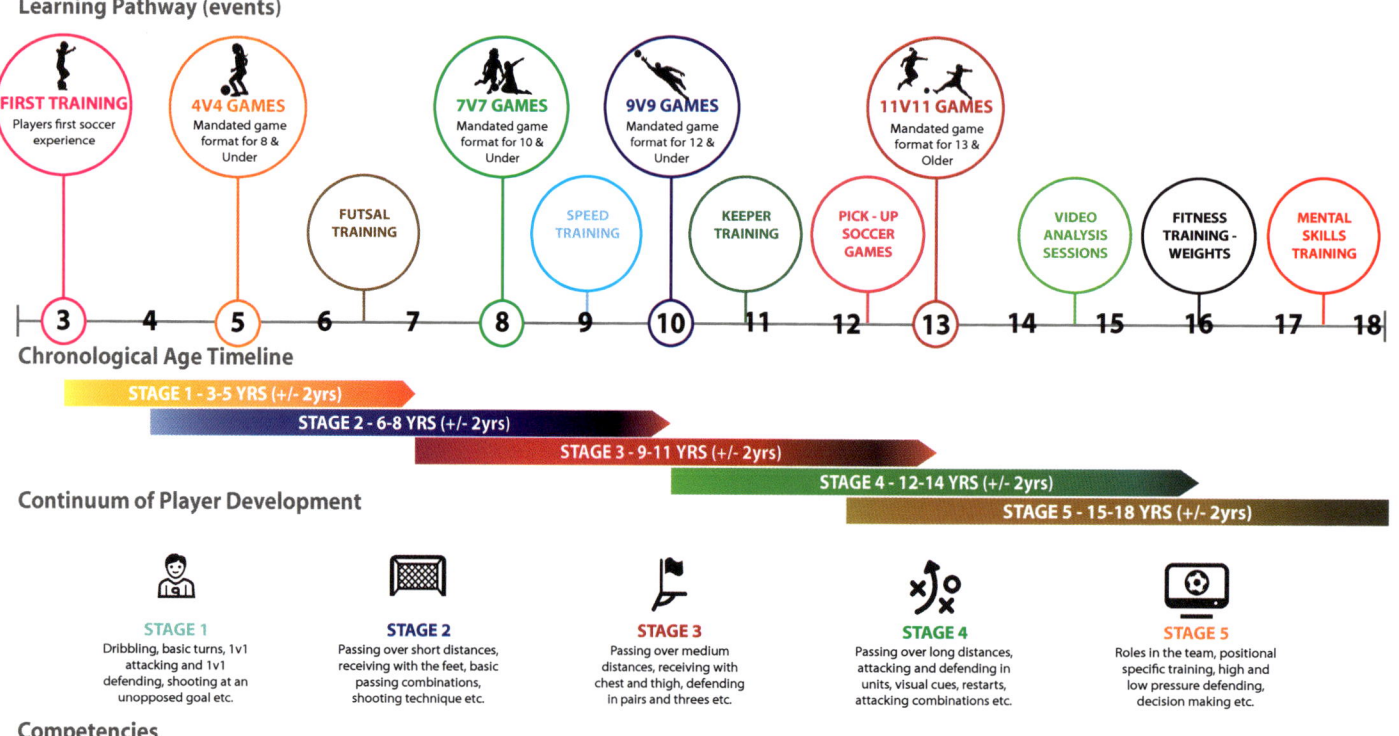

prepare coaches for this transition. The line has been drawn on the learning pathway to indicate when players should graduate to the next level of complexity – whether the players and coaches are ready or not.

Adopting a long term perspective is imperative. Establishing clear performance expectations and providing a detailed road map directing players and coaches along the youth soccer journey is vital. The proficiency of players will very much determine when the coach can transition the team. Ideally the coach can commence transition work with players at least 12 months prior to stepping to the next game format by layering in more demanding technical and tactical concepts. This can all be achieved by training in small groups and units without requiring the coach to introduce a full complement of players on the field.

Holistic View of Youth Soccer Experience

Holistic planning by the club and coaches is needed to increase the probability of a seamlessly transition for players, teams and coaches along the development continuum and learning pathway. A comprehensive player development curriculum building programs on principles that respect the developmental needs of all children is required.

The diagram on the previous page illustrates how the Learning Pathway and Player Development Continuum interrelate. An holistic approach for a player commencing soccer age 3 will account for 15 years of development before the child enters adulthood. A series of events are mapped along the Learning Pathway - some, such as the small sided games formats are determined by age and others, such as goalkeeper training or speed and agility, can be associated with the individual's readiness. We can then layer in the player development continuum to account for the fluidity in physical, mental and emotional maturity of players. The challenge coaches and administrators face is to determine where the players are along the development continuum, identify which learning event is appropriate and then select content to keep children moving positively along the scale.

Coach Development Pathway

As previously mentioned, I believe the biggest beneficiaries of change should be the coaches. An in-house coaching education program designed to regularly engage coaches in short duration and convenient training is the duty of youth clubs seriously committed to providing children with a supreme soccer experience. Coaches, like players, should have a learning pathway - a pathway mirroring the player development continuum and pathway - see image below. This is an ideal time for organizations lacking a coaching education

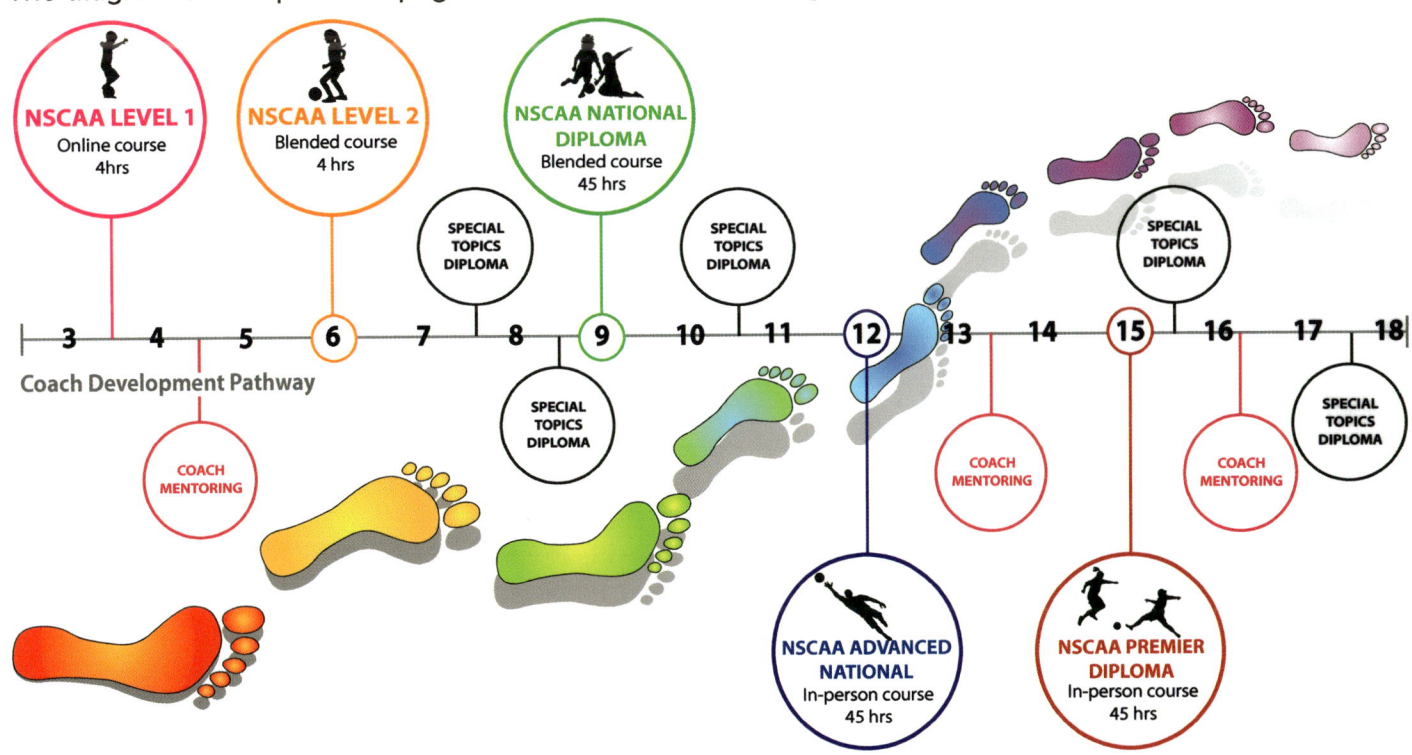

program that follows the player development continuum to establish one. An option is to institute a syllabus based on the Principles of Play.

The Principles of Play

The Principles of Play, attack and defense, are the underpinning concepts of the game and are applicable no matter what game format or level of participation. The Principles can be coached from a child's entry point to soccer and understanding the Principles of Play will enable a coach to plan for player and team development. The principles relate to attacking and defending and should not be confused with systems of play – the formation of the team on the field. The Principles of Play are the same in any system of play. Coaches with a working understanding of these principles make better decisions on which skill, technique and tactic to select. Depending on your frame of reference, the number and organization of the principles may vary, but for the purpose of this presentation, NSCAA identifies 5 principles of attack and defense, namely:

Attacking

1. Penetration
2. Width
3. Depth
4. Mobility
5. Improvisation

Defending

1. Pressure
2. Cover
3. Balance
4. Compactness
5. Patience/discipline/restraint

Considering Attacking and Defending Principles of Play encompass all age groups and game formats, deciding to adopt the Principles of Play as a guide for content development is reasonable. Becoming a proficient attacking and defending team requires competent individual play and progresses to small groups and teamwork. This longitudinal approach to technical and tactical development assists coaches in the transition of players from one learning event to another.

Conclusion

Major changes to the way we administer, coach and play soccer in USA have arrived. These changes bring with them great optimism for player development and coach education, but failure to plan for change will inevitably lead to missed opportunities.

I still believe there are many questions U.S. Soccer, leagues and clubs must address as we prepare our coaches, players and families for a 'new dawn in youth soccer' Here are 10 more worth considering:

1. What milestones will US Soccer introduced to measure the impact on the game and effectiveness of the initiatives?
2. What will be the consequence for clubs failing to embrace change?
3. What oversight will US Soccer utilize?
4. What strategies are in place to help clubs maintain and grow player and coach participation?
5. At what point do reduced sized fields lead to having less technical players as a result of coaches playing 'a get it forward and press' approach?
6. How is moving to a calendar year going to 'combat the relative age effects'? Haven't the goal posts just shifted?
7. How do we recover from cutting too many younger players (born March-July) from competitive A and B teams?
8. How will early developing children born between August and December fair as they transition from being the oldest to the youngest players in the reshuffle?
9. If an intended outcome is to keep players playing small sided games longer, how can it be the case that children in locations with Fall-Spring leagues will lose a year of small sided games?
10. Should US Soccer legislate leagues to move in line with age groupings and go to calendar years?

If you would like to continue your interest in this coaching education topic you may wish to receive the latest news and updates:
- NSCAA.com/elearning – courses & resources.
- ussoccer.com – Coaching Education – details about SSG mandates and initiatives.
- Fifa.com – Grassroots section
- usyouthsoccer.org – Small Sided Games – National Standards document (PDF)

SOCCER LEARNING PATHWAY DISCUSSION DOCUMENT

The purpose of this document is to offer some useful questions to support youth organizations seeking to implement or update a Learning Pathway. Print off copies of this page and distribute to members of the leadership team ahead of the next Board Meeting.

Philosophy, Aims, Goals and Outcomes

Of up-most importance for a youth education organization are statements defining the purpose, aims and anticipated learning outcomes. Once defined the philosophy can be taught and disseminated to Members and provide direction for all decision making:

1. Does the organization have a philosophy statement?
2. Is there a common belief between members of the leadership team and coaches how to organize experiences to maximize learning?
3. Is the philosophy statement written with sufficient clarity to guide the leadership team to extrapolate detail when creating club policies? For example, one would expect to find a 'Playing-up policy' encouraging player movement between age groups supporting a philosophy that supports ability-based grouping.

Program Structure

Defines the ideal sequence of learning experiences to reach the competency goals of the program? This is the What, Where, and How – the design of learning activities and programs.

4. Does the club have an education framework – a curriculum?
5. Is there a corresponding coach development learning pathway correlated to the player learning pathway preparing coaches to implement programming?
6. Are specific learning goals and competencies defined at different stages/ages to guide the selection of appropriate activities for players?
7. Is there a transition plan to progress players from one stage/learning experience to another? Such as the transition from 4v4 to 7v7 small sided game formats.
8. Do programming options vary for different levels of play? Such as recreation, competitive and elite.
9. Can the learner (or learner's parents) decide the appropriate development pathway to pursue based on commitment or competence, or will does the coach/club define the learning pathway?

Implementation and Evaluation

10. Does the club presume to provide all soccer learning experiences or are there expectations the learner will work at home independently and/or seek supplemental training outside of the club?
11. Who will evaluate the quality of programming and the efficacy of the learning pathway?
12. Can the club establish a 'learning pathway' sub-committee and what types of talented individuals are needed?
13. How will the club communicate to the Membership features and benefits of the soccer learning pathway?
14. What external support, if any, is needed to support the club in conceiving and implementing the learning pathway?

Is your organization ready? Ideally, the leadership team should be able to answer each question individually and collectively with consistent responses. Common strengths of high performing youth soccer clubs identified by the NSCAA include clear and well defined development philosophy, integrated programs and processes designed to raise coaching performance and the involvement of individuals with excellent appreciation how to construct learning pathways for players and coaches.

NSCAA offers a Consultation service via the NSCAA Club Standards Project to help youth organizations to prepare for the small sided games mandates and maximize opportunities to upgrade player and coach development programs. Contact David Newbery, NSCAA Club Standards Project Coordinator - dnewbery@nscaa.com or call 401-377-7008.

ABOUT THE NSCAA PLAYER DEVELOPMENT CURRICULUM

Theory of Player Development

The NSCAA approach emphasizes development-appropriate skill acquisition to maximize the player's potential. The supporting theory supports ever more complex and demanding conditions placed on the player as they advance through several stages of development, which include pre-puberty, puberty, post-puberty and maturation. In addition to physical transformations, the model also accounts for changes in emotional and cognitive development, factors having a dramatic effect on the capacity of players to learn and perform. Significant developmental differences also exist between children of the same gender and same age. To this end NSCAA model supports the adage – "if you are good enough ... you are old enough". It is extremely important to offer programming flexibility to enable each child to find their training and performance level. This perspective should not only apply to 'playing-up', but also to placing players 'down'. Our focus must always be on what is best for the child – a decision involving a number of variables. One reason players plateau and leave soccer is an overemphasis on competition instead of training during the important period in their athletic development. Stage 1, 2 and 3 are the most important phases of preparation, physically, mentally, emotionally and in the development of key soccer skills of dribbling, passing and control.

Stages of Development

Originally a model for Elite Athlete Development, the NSCAA pathway provides a process for development from early childhood through retirement. Stage 1 (4 and 5 year olds), Stage 2 (6-8), Stage 3 (9-11), Stage 4 (12-14) and Stage 5 (15-18). Each stage of the model promotes a different development focus – the interplay between physical, cognitive, emotional, psychological and social variables. For example, when working with four and five year olds consider that players of this age tire easily, need repetition and reinforcement, have short attention span and mostly approach tasks individually.

In terms of soccer participation, we need to ensure the sessions are short, activities change constantly, skills are demonstrated and continually reinforced and information needs to be camouflaged and concealed, such as using cartoon characters and creating a story for a particular activity. Importantly, every child should have a ball at their feet for the vast majority of time. Team play at this stage of development should be restricted to small sided games and 1v1 situations. As players move into Stage 2 we start introducing passing and working cooperatively with teammates.

Competency Based Coaching

Regardless of the age and ability of players, a 'Player Development' Coach should be focused on nurturing children to achieve end of stage goals and attainment targets. To this end, NSCAA supports a 'competency' based approach to player development. On the next few pages, the Competency Matrix provides benchmarks for performance. Competency is the relationship between skill, selection and application of skills, tactics, strategies and ideas and the readiness of body and mind to cope with the activity. The NSCAA Player Development Curriculum considers skill development as a progressive process – meaning, competency in basic skills must be achieved before progressing to more complex skills. The Competency Matrix guides coaches to understand when it is appropriate to introduce players to a skill and when players should be expected to demonstrate a level of proficiency (competence).

COMPETENCY MATRIX

Stage of Development	Stage 1			Stage 2			Stage 3			Stage 4			Stage 5			
Age in years	3	4	5	6	7	8	9	10	11	12	13	14	15	16	17	18
PHYSICAL LITERACY SKILLS																
Run with stops and starts	−			+												
Run and change directions	−			+												
Gallop	−			+												
Skip	−			+												
Lateral movements - side-step	−			+												
Rolling, bending low, arching	−			+												
Balance - on a line	−			+												
Balance - on one foot	−			+												
Throw - strong hand	−				+											
Throw - weak hand	−				+											
Jump - make shapes in air	−		+													
Jump - one foot to another	−		+													
Jump - stride and bound patterns	−						+									
Jump - hurdles	−						+									
Quick feet and crossovers		−			+											
Speed - Coordination of arms and legs					−					+						
Speed - explosive first step						−				+						
Running technique		−								+						
Sprinting technique						−				+						
DRIBBLING SKILLS																
Turns - basic	−			+												
Turns - advanced				−			+									
Dribbling basics	−			+												

Competency based coaching: this approach suggests performance improvements are acquired progressively – meaning, competency in basic skills/knowledge must be achieved before progressing to more complex skills and concepts. With this in mind, the Competency Matrix helps coaches to know when players should be 'Introduced' (−) to a skill/concept and when players should be expected to demonstrate 'Competency' (+).

© ALL RIGHTS RESERVED - COACHING MEDIA GROUP AND NSCAA

COMPETENCY MATRIX

Stage of Development	Stage 1			Stage 2			Stage 3			Stage 4			Stage 5			
Age in years	3	4	5	6	7	8	9	10	11	12	13	14	15	16	17	18
DRIBBLING SKILLS CONTINUED																
Running with the ball				-			+									
Feints and dribble		-						+								
Beating an opponent			-					+								
Escaping an opponent			-					+								
RECEIVING																
Control - Foot			-							+						
Control - Thigh					-						+					
Control - Chest						-						+				
Control - Head						-						+				
PASSING																
Ground - Inside of foot - 5 yards				-			+									
Ground - Inside of foot - 10 yards					-				+							
Ground - Inside of foot - 20 yards						-					+					
Ground - Instep						-				+						
Long pass						-						+				
Chip/Lofted pass							-					+				
Swerve pass - inside of foot							-					+				
Swerve pass - outside of foot							-					+				
Crossing							-					+				
SHOOTING																
Instep			-						+							
Half volley						-					+					
Volley						-					+					

Competency based coaching: this approach suggests performance improvements are acquired progressively – meaning, competency in basic skills/knowledge must be achieved before progressing to more complex skills and concepts. With this in mind, the Competency Matrix helps coaches to know when players should be 'Introduced' (-) to a skill/concept and when players should be expected to demonstrate 'Competency' (+).

COMPETENCY MATRIX

Stage of Development	Stage 1			Stage 2			Stage 3			Stage 4			Stage 5			
Age in years	3	4	5	6	7	8	9	10	11	12	13	14	15	16	17	18
SHOOTING CONTINUED																
One on one with Goal Keeper								-					+			
HEADING																
Basic technique				-							+					
Defensive header								-					+			
Attacking header								-					+			
PHYSICAL CONDITIONING																
Own body weight strength exercises								-								+
Core body strength								-								+
Dynamic warm-up						-										+
Flexibility							-									+
Aerobic Endurance training										-						+
Anaerobic Endurance training										-						+
Speed training (Anaerobic)										-						+
MENTAL/COGNITIVE CONDITIONING																
Confidence	-												+			
Commitment							-						+			
Concentration	-												+			
Composure							-									+
GOAL KEEPING																
Basic Catching Techniques					-					+						
Positioning							-				+					
Diving								-					+			
Distribution								-					+			

Competency based coaching: this approach suggests performance improvements are acquired progressively – meaning, competency in basic skills/knowledge must be achieved before progressing to more complex skills and concepts. With this in mind, the Competency Matrix helps coaches to know when players should be 'Introduced' (-) to a skill/concept and when players should be expected to demonstrate 'Competency' (+).

COMPETENCY MATRIX

Stage of Development	Stage 1			Stage 2			Stage 3			Stage 4			Stage 5			
Age in years	3	4	5	6	7	8	9	10	11	12	13	14	15	16	17	18
GOAL KEEPING CONTINUED																
Advanced Techniques - crosses, punching etc										-						+
SET PLAYS																
Throw in				-				+								
Penalties				-						+						
Corners				-										+		
Goal Kicks				-						+						
Free Kicks				-										+		
ATTACKING PRINCIPLES AND TECHNIQUES																
Attacking as an individual 1v1		-										+				
Attacking in pairs (2v1 and 2v2)				-								+				
Attacking in small groups (3's and 4's)							-							+		
Attacking as a unit and team								-								+
Support with and without the ball						-							+			
Attacking from wide positions								-						+		
Crossing balls into the penalty box								-						+		
Transition and counter attacks							-									+
Finishing						-										+
Attacking set plays									-							+
Communication							-									+
Positional Play							-									+
DEFENSIVE PRINCIPLES AND TECHNIQUES																
Defending as an individual 1v1 - pressure				-						+						
Defending in pairs (2v1 and 2v2) - pressure and cover						-						+				

Competency based coaching: this approach suggests performance improvements are acquired progressively – meaning, competency in basic skills/knowledge must be achieved before progressing to more complex skills and concepts. With this in mind, the Competency Matrix helps coaches to know when players should be 'Introduced' (-) to a skill/concept and when players should be expected to demonstrate 'Competency' (+).

COMPETENCY MATRIX

Stage of Development	Stage 1			Stage 2			Stage 3			Stage 4			Stage 5			
Age in years	3	4	5	6	7	8	9	10	11	12	13	14	15	16	17	18
DEFENSIVE PRINCIPLES AND TECHNIQUES CONTINUED																
Defending in small groups (3's and 4's) - pressure, cover, balance									−					+		
Defending as a unit and team										−						+
Marking								−					+			
Recovery								−				+				
Communication								−						+		
Transition from defense to attack								−								+
Defensive set plays									−				+			
Positional Play								−								+
LAWS OF THE GAME																
Individual and Team Behavior	−									+						
Field and Equipment		−								+						
Restarts				−			+									
Fair and foul play	−									+						
Basic Rules	−					+										
Free kicks - offside, direct and indirect etc				−						+						
Misc laws - advantage etc						−				+						

Competency based coaching: this approach suggests performance improvements are acquired progressively – meaning, competency in basic skills/knowledge must be achieved before progressing to more complex skills and concepts. With this in mind, the Competency Matrix helps coaches to know when players should be 'Introduced' (−) to a skill/concept and when players should be expected to demonstrate 'Competency' (+).

ACTIVITIES LISTING

Introduction activities
14 Numbers Passing
15 Countdown
16 Attacking Fullbacks
17 Flying Fullbacks
18 Center Midfield Link-up and Finishing 5v3
19 Four Goal Game

4v4 Formations
21 4v4 Formations - 0-1-2-1
22 4v4 Formations - 0-2-2
23 4v4 Formations - 0-1-3

4v4 Activities
24 Wall Pass Functional
25 Wall Pass Phase of Play
26 Wall Pass the Game
27 Pressure & cover defending Functional
28 Pressure and Cover defending Phase
29 Pressure and Cover defending Game
30 Attacking with Width Functional
31 Attacking with Width Phase
32 Attacking with Width Game
33 Defensive Stop with Attacking Transition Functional
34 Defensive Stop with Attacking Transition Phase
35 Defensive Stop with Attacking Transition Game

7v7 Formations
37 7v7 Formations - 1-2-1-3
38 7v7 Formations - 1-3-1-2
39 7v7 Formations - 1-3-2-1

7v7 Activities
40 4v2 to 4v4 Attacking width - functional
41 5v3 to 5v6 attacking width - phase of play
42 7v7 Attacking Width Game
43 Penetration 6v3 to 6v6 Functional
44 Penetration 5v4 Through Around or Over Phase
45 Penetration 7v7 Through Around or Over Game
46 1v1 to 2v2 Pressure and Cover Defending - Functional
47 4v4 Pressure, Cover, Balance Defending - Phase
48 7v7 Pressure, Cover, Balance Defending - Game
49 4v3 to 5v5 defending in small groups - functional
50 6v7 defending in small groups - phase
51 7v7 defending in small groups - Game

9v9 Formations
53 9v9 Formations - 1-4-3-1
54 9v9 Formations - 1-2-3-3
55 9v9 Formations - 1-2-4-2

9v9 Activities
56 9v9 Creating Space in the Final Third 1
57 9v9 Creating Space in the Final Third 2
58 Creating Space IN 9v9 game
59 Defensive organization back 4
60 Defensive organization Midfield 3
61 Defensive organization high pressure
62 Switching the point of attack
63 9v9 Attacking the weak-side
64 9v9 Patience in Attack
65 4v3 to 4v4 Midfield Pressure and Counter Attack
66 Defending 8v8 plus 1
67 9v9 Low Pressure Defending

NUMBERS PASSING

Why use it?
A terrific unopposed introductory passing activity can be employed with equally great effect with 6 and 18 year old players. Intensity can be increased - fast!

Set up
20x20 yards. 8-10 players randomly space themselves in the area. The coach gives each player a number, i.e. 1, 2, 3 .... 9, 10. One ball starts with player 1.

How to play
'Walk through' the activity with the players for 1-2 sequences. If needed, rehearse the activity by passing the ball with the hands using a basketball style chest pass. Pass the ball from one teammate to another in number order - i.e. 1 passes to 2, 2 to 3 etc. When 10 receives the pass from 9, 10 passes to 1 and the routine starts again. Begin with unlimited touches and then restrict to 2 touch or eventually, 1 touch. At first, expect players to stand flat-footed, unsure where to move. This is your teaching moment! In addition to coaching short and medium length passing, the coach can also teach movement and creating space. Instruct the players to move away from the ball after they have made a pass, look for space. With more advanced players have them 'look over their shoulder' to locate space with the first touch. Once the group has established a rhythm, instruct players they must run through a corner gate before re-entering the area - always watching the play as they run to the corner.

Coaching notes
Coaching Objectives: Passers should concentrate on first touch away from pressure and a firm pass on the ground to feet or space. Receiver should attempt to get in front of the passer to prevent the passers need to turn. Communication - call names or numbers.
Coaching Tips: Freeze the play to allow players to see space - ask them to move to a better position and restart.

How to modify
Less Challenging: Pass the ball with the hands, reduce the number of players, increase the space.
More Challenging: Add 2-3 balls, players run through corner gates, 1 touch quickens the pace, split the group into 2-3 teams working in the same area, add a double pass combination.

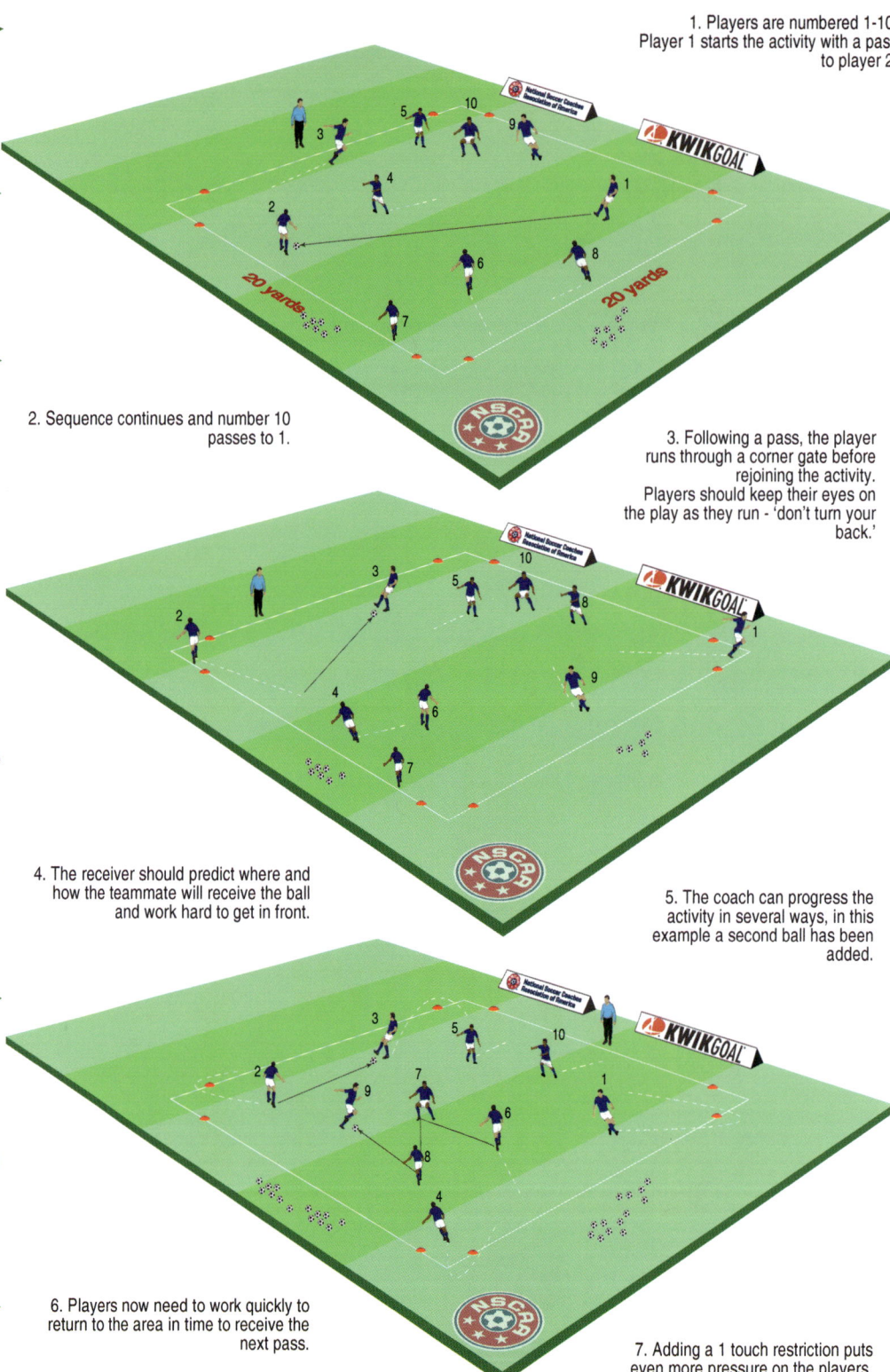

1. Players are numbered 1-10. Player 1 starts the activity with a pass to player 2.

2. Sequence continues and number 10 passes to 1.

3. Following a pass, the player runs through a corner gate before rejoining the activity. Players should keep their eyes on the play as they run - 'don't turn your back.'

4. The receiver should predict where and how the teammate will receive the ball and work hard to get in front.

5. The coach can progress the activity in several ways, in this example a second ball has been added.

6. Players now need to work quickly to return to the area in time to receive the next pass.

7. Adding a 1 touch restriction puts even more pressure on the players.

Stage/s of development covered by activity
Stages 2, 3, 4 & 5 - 6-18 year old players.

Development themes and competencies
Top 3 Themes: Passing over short and medium distances, creating space and communication.
Top 3 Competencies: Passing, receiving and support with and without the ball.

COUNTDOWN

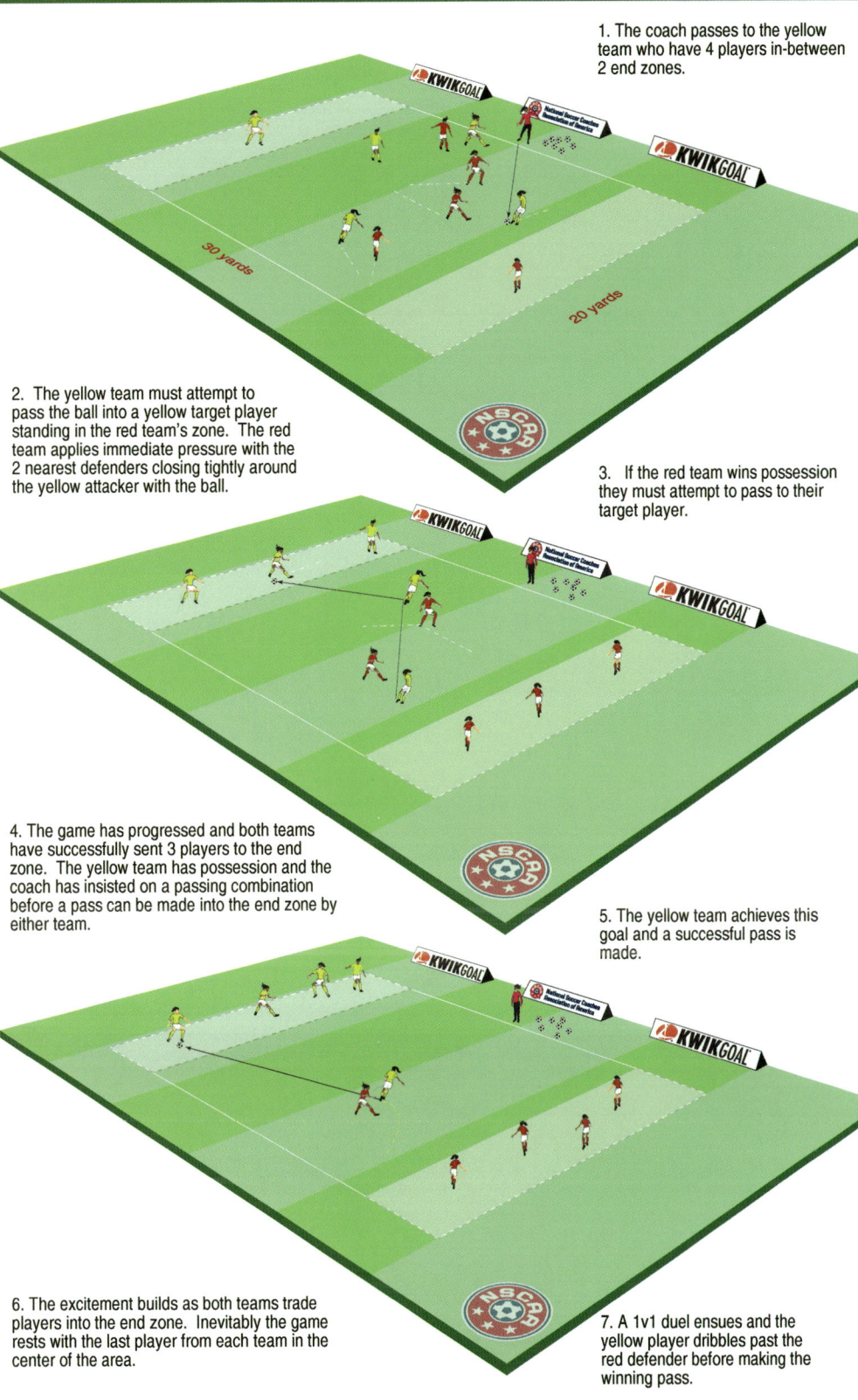

1. The coach passes to the yellow team who have 4 players in-between 2 end zones.

2. The yellow team must attempt to pass the ball into a yellow target player standing in the red team's zone. The red team applies immediate pressure with the 2 nearest defenders closing tightly around the yellow attacker with the ball.

3. If the red team wins possession they must attempt to pass to their target player.

4. The game has progressed and both teams have successfully sent 3 players to the end zone. The yellow team has possession and the coach has insisted on a passing combination before a pass can be made into the end zone by either team.

5. The yellow team achieves this goal and a successful pass is made.

6. The excitement builds as both teams trade players into the end zone. Inevitably the game rests with the last player from each team in the center of the area.

7. A 1v1 duel ensues and the yellow player dribbles past the red defender before making the winning pass.

Why use it?

Countdown is a very popular game with the players as it is fast paced and exciting. As the number of players on both teams start to dwindle the importance of decision making increases.

Set up

The area is a 30x20 yards rectangle with a 5 yards end zone marked at both ends. Two teams of 5 players nominate a target player to stand in the opponents end zone and the remaining players spread out in between the zones. The coach stands on the sideline with a large supply of balls.

How to play

The objective of the game is to be the first team to have all players in the opponents end zone. To achieve that goal the players must combine passes with the target player. If the target player is able to control the ball and place their foot on top of the ball in the end zone, the player making the final pass joins the target player. If the ball leaves the area the coach restarts and makes a pass to the opposing team. Continue the sequence until the last player on either team makes the final pass to a target player. Play again.

Coaching notes

Coaching Objectives: There are numerous attacking and defending competencies that a coach can focus on in this activity. Defensive compactness to prevent penetrating passes into the target players and movement by players to create width are just a couple of objectives.
Coaching Tips: There are times in a training session the coach will just want to 'let the game be the teacher'. Once players understand the rules and objectives, give them the responsibility to work on their own tactics. Typically, discussions will occur on who to start as the target player and which player the team wants to be the last to pass.

How to modify

Less Challenging: Start with 2-3 target players to provide more room in between the zones.
More Challenging: Add a second ball, insist on a passing combination before passing to the target, introduce a touch restriction, if a ball leaves the field the team must send back a target player and change the shape of the field to create different challenges.

Stage/s of development covered by activity

Stages 2, 3 & 4 - 6-14 year old players.

Development themes and competencies

Top 3 Themes: Passing over short and medium distances, support and defensive pressure.
Top 3 Competencies: Passing, receiving and 1v1 defending.

ATTACKING FULLBACKS

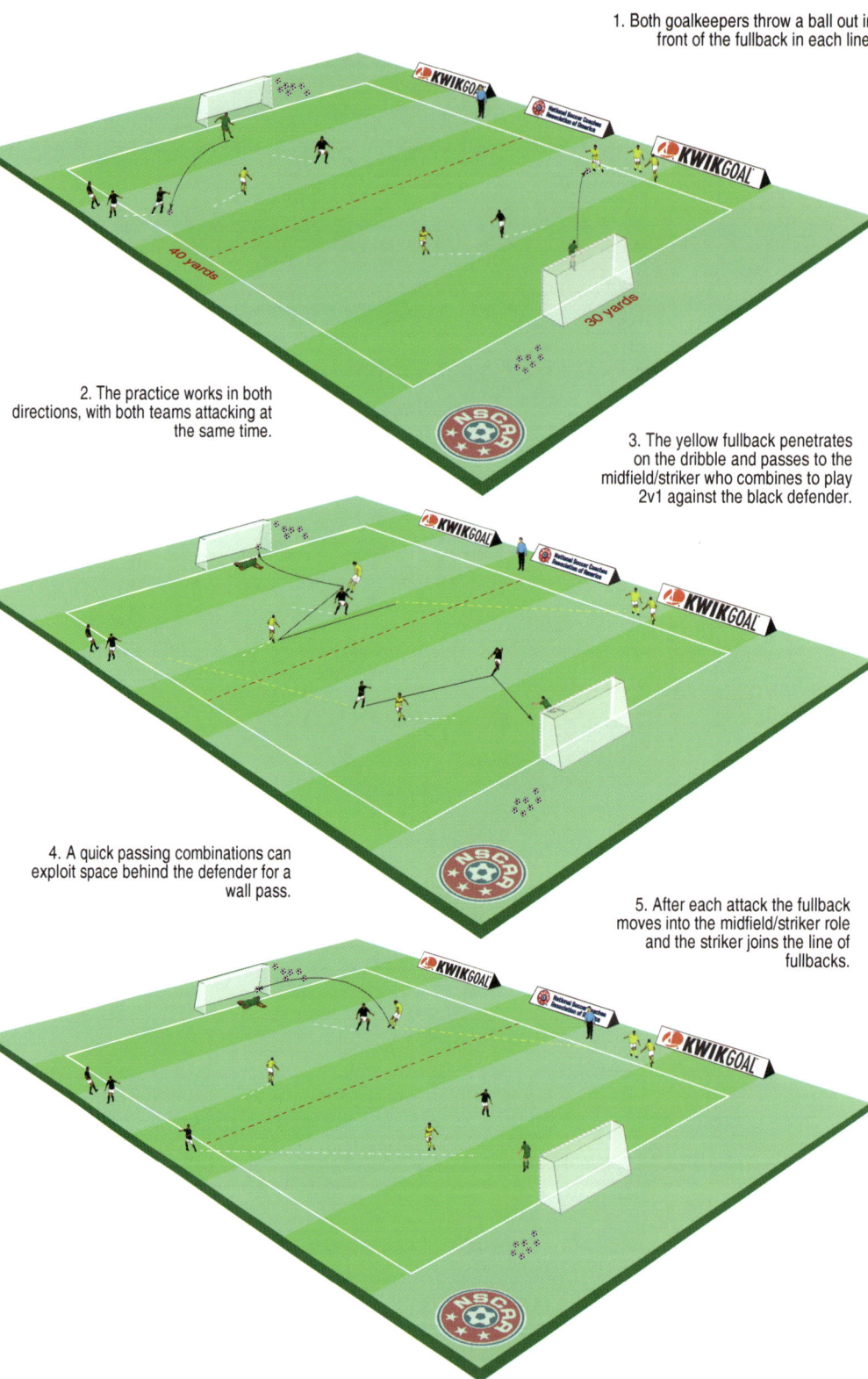

Why use it?
Developing patterns of play can be a good approach to help young players understand different roles on the field. More often than not, a pattern will be unopposed or semi opposed to give the players time and space. In 'Attacking Fullbacks' we focussed on combination play between goalkeeper defender and midfield - a good way to develop play from the backline forward.

Set up
The area is 40x30 yards with an appropriate size goal at each end of the field. There are 10 outfield players and 2 goalkeepers and in each half of the field an attacking midfield/striker and a defender waits for play to develop. The goalkeepers have a large supply of balls and a group of 3 attacking fullbacks set up on the sideline approximately 10 yards from each end line.

How to play
Play is developed from both ends of the field simultaneously, commencing with a throw or pass from the goalkeeper to the first fullback in the line. On receipt of the ball the fullback must penetrate on the dribble to engage the defender. A midfield/forward player supports the fullback on the 'inside' of the defender, so the fullback can decide to combine with the midfield player or attempt a shot.

Coaching notes
Coaching Objectives: The primary objective is to develop play from the goalkeeper to the fullback and then link-up play with the midfield player.
Coaching Tips: The starting position and depth of the fullback players is important. The angle from the goal should be sufficiently shallow to allow the goalkeeper to throw the ball ahead of the fullback who is facing up-field. The fullback should have an open body shape on receipt of the ball to enable the player's first touch to quickly exploit attacking space. Realistic to the game, the support midfield player should stay central and allow the fullback space wide to penetrate on the dribble.

How to modify
Less Challenging: Start the activity without the defender to develop confidence and understanding.
More Challenging: Dribbling is one option to build out of the back – the coach can also require a pass to the midfield player inside. Various passing combinations can be introduced, such as a wall pass, overlap or a double pass.

1. Both goalkeepers throw a ball out in front of the fullback in each line.
2. The practice works in both directions, with both teams attacking at the same time.
3. The yellow fullback penetrates on the dribble and passes to the midfield/striker who combines to play 2v1 against the black defender.
4. A quick passing combinations can exploit space behind the defender for a wall pass.
5. After each attack the fullback moves into the midfield/striker role and the striker joins the line of fullbacks.

Stage/s of development covered by activity
Stages 3, 4 & 5 - 9-18 year old players.

Development themes and competencies
Top 3 Themes: Passing over short and medium distances, passing combinations and building play from the defense.
Top 3 Competencies: Passing, receiving and support with and without the ball.

FLYING FULLBACKS

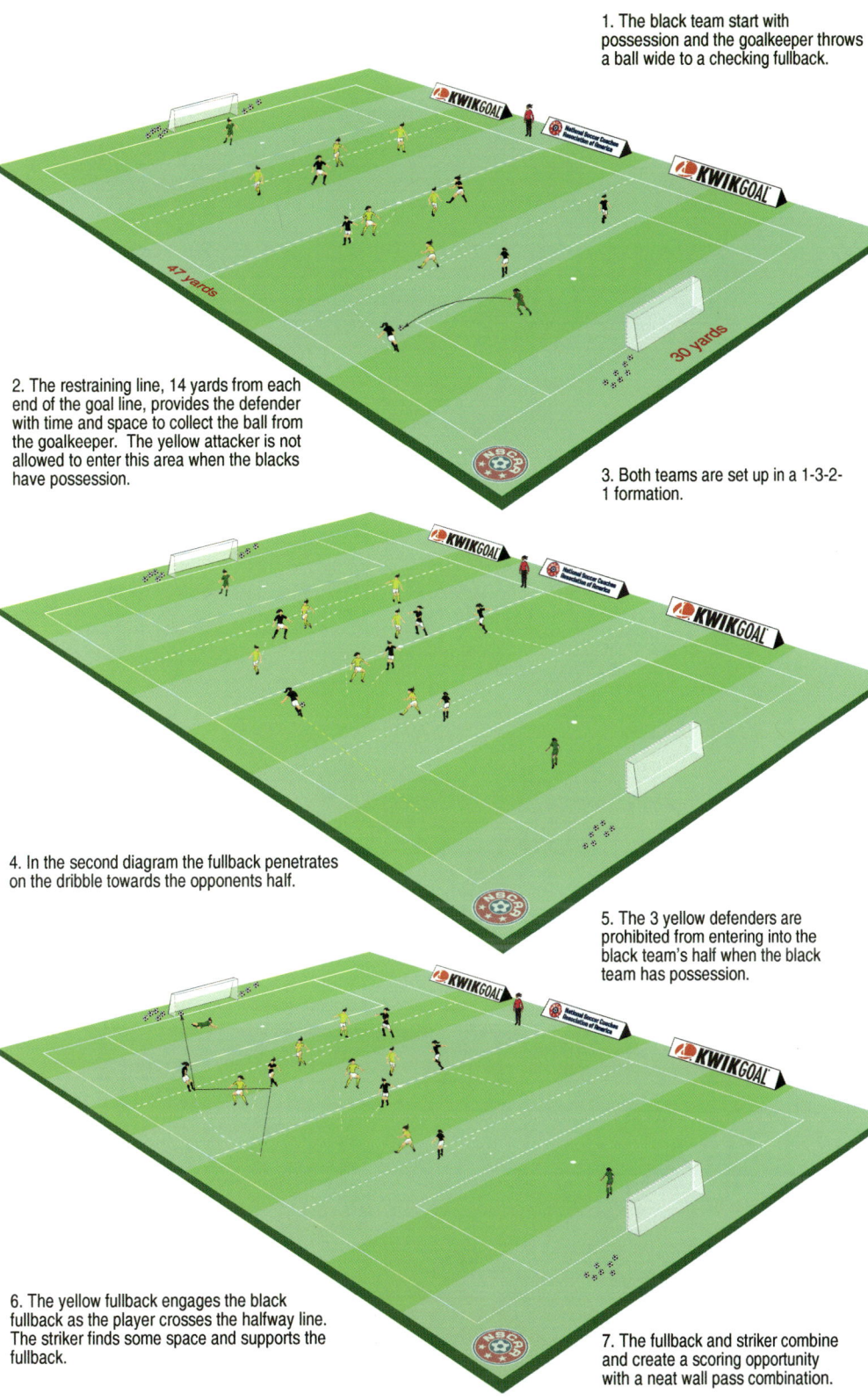

1. The black team start with possession and the goalkeeper throws a ball wide to a checking fullback.

2. The restraining line, 14 yards from each end of the goal line, provides the defender with time and space to collect the ball from the goalkeeper. The yellow attacker is not allowed to enter this area when the blacks have possession.

3. Both teams are set up in a 1-3-2-1 formation.

4. In the second diagram the fullback penetrates on the dribble towards the opponents half.

5. The 3 yellow defenders are prohibited from entering into the black team's half when the black team has possession.

6. The yellow fullback engages the black fullback as the player crosses the halfway line. The striker finds some space and supports the fullback.

7. The fullback and striker combine and create a scoring opportunity with a neat wall pass combination.

Why use it?
This session provides opportunities to practice different attacking scenarios requiring the goalkeeper and fullbacks to take an active part in building an attack. It gives you an opportunity to work with the goalkeeper, defense and midfield players to build up an attack from defensive positions.

Set up
The activity is played on a 7v7 small sided game field approximately 47x30 yards and appropriate size goals are at each end. The goal keepers have a supply of balls next to the goal and restart each time the ball leaves the field. The natural markings of the field provide a restraining line to enable the defenders to bring the ball out of the backfield.

How to play
To begin, the coach can add some game conditions to provide the fullbacks with the best chance of success. It is also important to set the team up in a formation encouraging the theme, so in this case we set up both teams with a goalkeeper, 3 defenders, 2 central midfield players and a striker. As before, the goalkeeper has a supply of balls next to the goal to restart play. The coach uses the markings on the field to create a restraining line 14 yards from each goal and only the 3 defensive players can enter the end zone when their goalkeeper has possession. When the opponent has the ball, the 3 defenders are restricted from entering the opponent's end of the field. The objective is for the goalkeeper to start the play with a serve to either fullback and for the team to progress the ball through the lines of the field.

Coaching notes
Coaching Objectives: The defensive and midfield units must work with the goalkeeper to play the ball forward to the striker. On receipt of the ball by the goalkeeper, wide defensive players and wide midfield players should stretch the field wide
Coaching Tips: Consistent with the 'Attacking Fullbacks' activity, the fullbacks must get wide and deep when the goalkeeper has possession. Preventing the opposing players entering into the end zone ensures the goalkeeper always has an option to build play through the fullbacks. This is now a rule of the new 7v7 small sided game format in USA.

How to modify
Less Challenging: The restraining line also provides the fullbacks with a visual cue so they know how deep the coach wants them to support the goalkeeper. Restricting opposing defenders entering the other teams half also provides the attacking team with a numerical advantage – 6v3 in most cases.
More Challenging: Once the attacking teams are achieving success, start to lift the restrictions.

Stage/s of development covered by activity
Stages 3, 4 & 5 - 9-18 year old players.

Development themes and competencies
Top 3 Themes: Passing over short and medium distances, passing combinations and building play from the defense.
Top 3 Competencies: Passing, receiving and support with and without the ball.

CENTER MIDFIELD LINK-UP AND FINISHING 5V3

Why use it?
As young players start to develop a proficiency in the basic techniques, coaches can start to work with players on positional roles and principles of play. In this activity our focus is on the link play between central midfield players and strikers and creating depth in attack.

Set up
A 40x30 yards area with 2 small goals at both ends of the field approximately 5 yards from the sidelines. Play 3v3 inside the area and 2 target players playing for the team in possession of the ball positioned off the end line and between the goals. The coach starts with the balls on the sideline.

How to play
In a 7v7, 9v9 and 11v11 game, coaches will often play with 1 or more central midfield players and strikers. Time is well spent on the training ground working on link play and emphasizing different types of passing combinations and movements off the ball. The coach starts the activity by playing a pass to either team in their defensive half of the field. The objective is for the attacking team to score in either of the 2 small goals. The attacking team has a striker positioned between the goals that should be used to maintain possession and establish triangle combinations with the 3 attackers. The defenders must attempt to win possession and counter attack using the numerical advantage - 5v3.

Coaching notes
Coaching Objectives: Work with the attacking team to use their numerical advantage and deep lying target players. Challenge the attacking team to play quickly to the unmarked striker and make runs off the ball to confuse the defense.
Coaching Tips: Playing with 4 lines - goalkeeper, defense, midfield and strikers - requires the team to develop depth (spreading the play vertically). With players in stage 3, in particular, the concept of depth is often hard to grasp, so the coach can impose conditions such as playing with a striker 'fixed' to the end line to establish depth.

How to modify
Less Challenging: Remove 1 of the defenders if the attackers are struggling to combine and score. Move the goals further apart to spread the defenders and give the striker more room to operate. Start the defenders in the defensive end.
More Challenging: Limit finishing touches to 1 touch, insist that before every goal the striker must touch the ball and add a condition that all 3 attackers must touch the ball before a goal is scored.

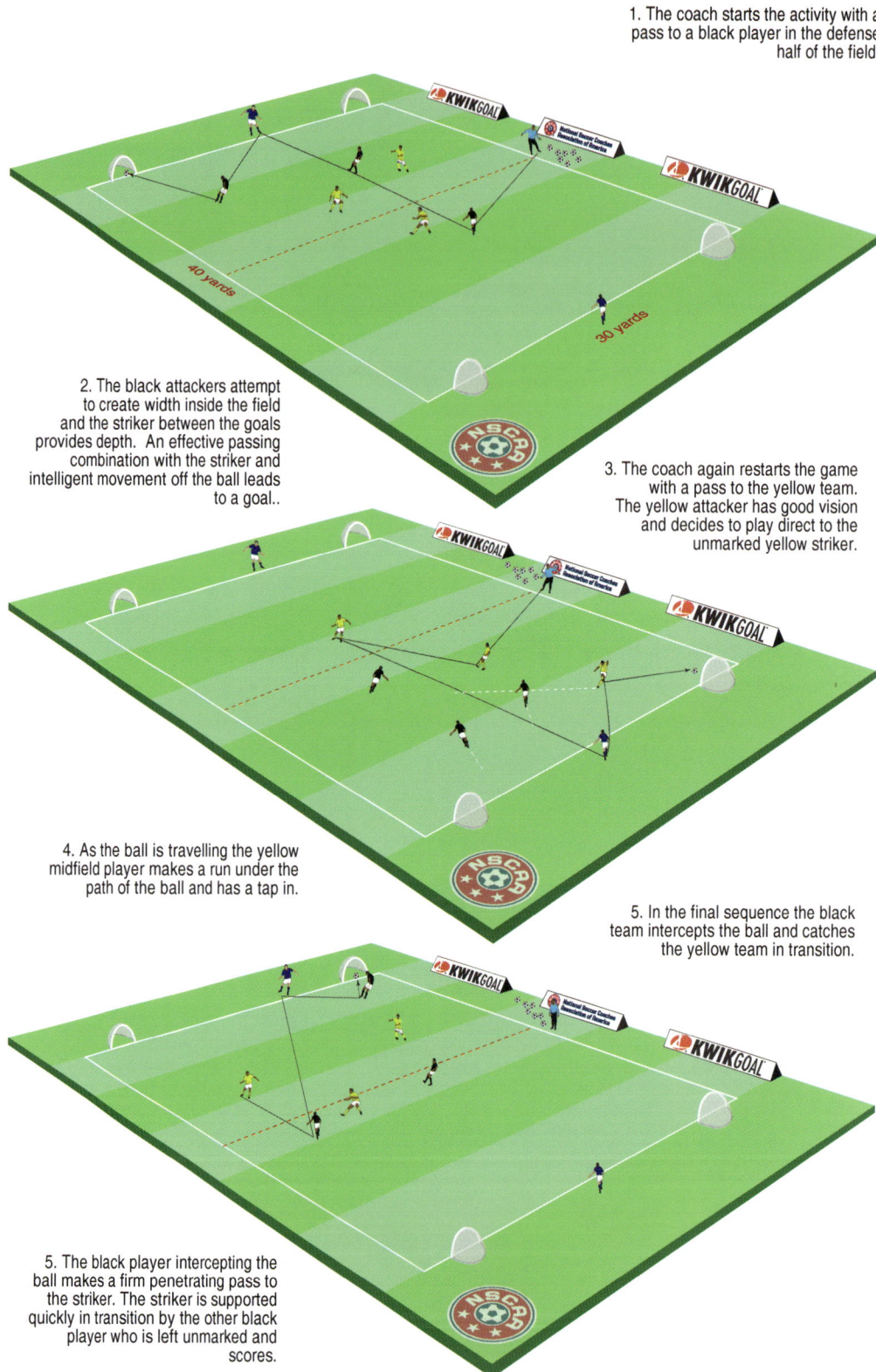

1. The coach starts the activity with a pass to a black player in the defense half of the field.

2. The black attackers attempt to create width inside the field and the striker between the goals provides depth. An effective passing combination with the striker and intelligent movement off the ball leads to a goal..

3. The coach again restarts the game with a pass to the yellow team. The yellow attacker has good vision and decides to play direct to the unmarked yellow striker.

4. As the ball is travelling the yellow midfield player makes a run under the path of the ball and has a tap in.

5. In the final sequence the black team intercepts the ball and catches the yellow team in transition.

5. The black player intercepting the ball makes a firm penetrating pass to the striker. The striker is supported quickly in transition by the other black player who is left unmarked and scores.

Stage/s of development covered by activity
Stages 3, 4 & 5 - 9-18 year old players.

Development themes and competencies
Top 3 Themes: Passing over short and medium distances, creating space and link play.
Top 3 Competencies: Passing and receiving, making support runs and defending pressure/cover.

FOUR GOAL GAME

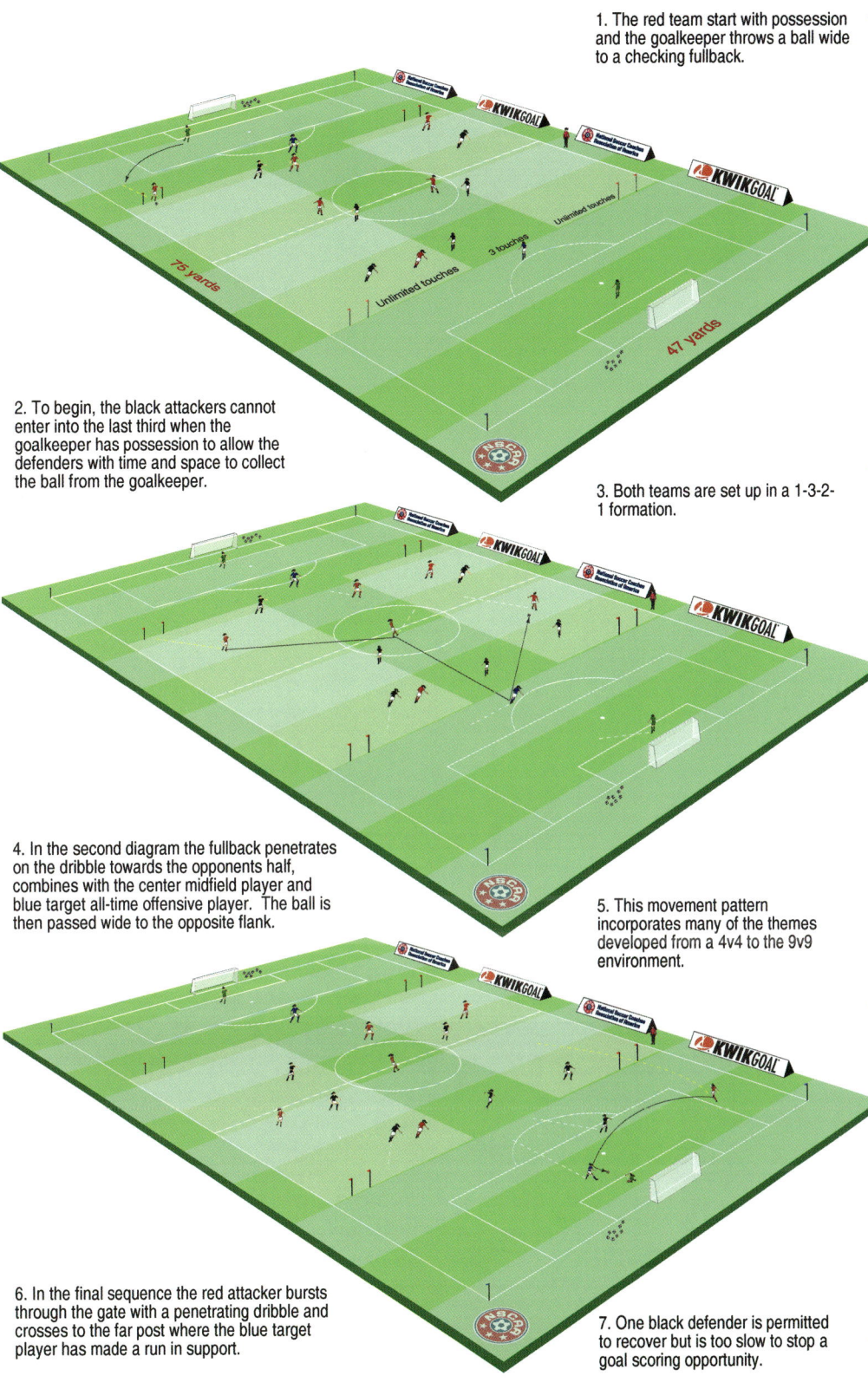

1. The red team start with possession and the goalkeeper throws a ball wide to a checking fullback.

2. To begin, the black attackers cannot enter into the last third when the goalkeeper has possession to allow the defenders with time and space to collect the ball from the goalkeeper.

3. Both teams are set up in a 1-3-2-1 formation.

4. In the second diagram the fullback penetrates on the dribble towards the opponents half, combines with the center midfield player and blue target all-time offensive player. The ball is then passed wide to the opposite flank.

5. This movement pattern incorporates many of the themes developed from a 4v4 to the 9v9 environment.

6. In the final sequence the red attacker bursts through the gate with a penetrating dribble and crosses to the far post where the blue target player has made a run in support.

7. One black defender is permitted to recover but is too slow to stop a goal scoring opportunity.

Why use it?
Having previously worked with the midfield players on link play with the defenders and attackers, we now move to the final activity encompassing the same themes played on the 9v9 field. Targets and restrictions in different areas provide an exciting challenge for players to overcome in this intense game.

Set up
This activity is played on a 9v9 full field approximately 75 x 47 yards, with 2 appropriate size goals at each end. The field is divided into thirds and the middle area is also subdivided into 3 zones. The players are allowed 3 touches in the middle zone and unlimited touches in wide positions. Flags are used to create wide zones and balls are placed next to each goal for restarts from the goalkeeper.

How to play
This activity provides a coach with many opportunities to coach attacking and defending concepts. The particular focus of this plan is developing play from the goalkeeper to strikers through the lines of the team. The target players are incorporated to create depth in-front and behind the midfield and the gates require the attacks to develop wide. Also, to familiarize the players with game conditions, the activity commences in the middle third of the field. The objective is for the team in possession to penetrate through the side gates and enter the attacking third of the opposing team. The advanced target player can move between the gates and the attacking team must aim to combine with the striker. If the attack is successful, the target player and the player penetrating through the gate can attempt to score against the goalkeeper and one defender from the midfield area can recover. By dividing the middle third in zones and introducing different touch restrictions the players are conditioned to change the rhythm of play

Coaching notes
Coaching Objectives: Use the field markings to orientate players and create game day conditions. The coach does not need to have all the players on the field for a full 9v9 game, but the positions should be realistic to the strategies employed in a game. Where appropriate try to tie-in connected themes and strategies. This activity enables a coach to include passing combinations through all 4 lines of the team.
Coaching Tips: Allow players to regain the team shape before serving another ball. The practice will have limited value if the players are out of position at the start.

How to modify
Less Challenging: Allow the fullbacks to enter into the defensive third unopposed to collect a pass from the goalkeeper.
More Challenging: To finish remove the flags and restrictions to see if the players can perform what they practiced in an unrestricted game. Add more players to both teams.

Stage/s of development covered by activity
Stages 3, 4 & 5 - 9-18 year old players.

Development themes and competencies
Top 3 Themes: Passing over short and medium distances, passing combinations and building play from the defense.
Top 3 Competencies: Passing, receiving and support with and without the ball.

4v4 FORMATIONS - 0-1-2-1

Attacking Shape

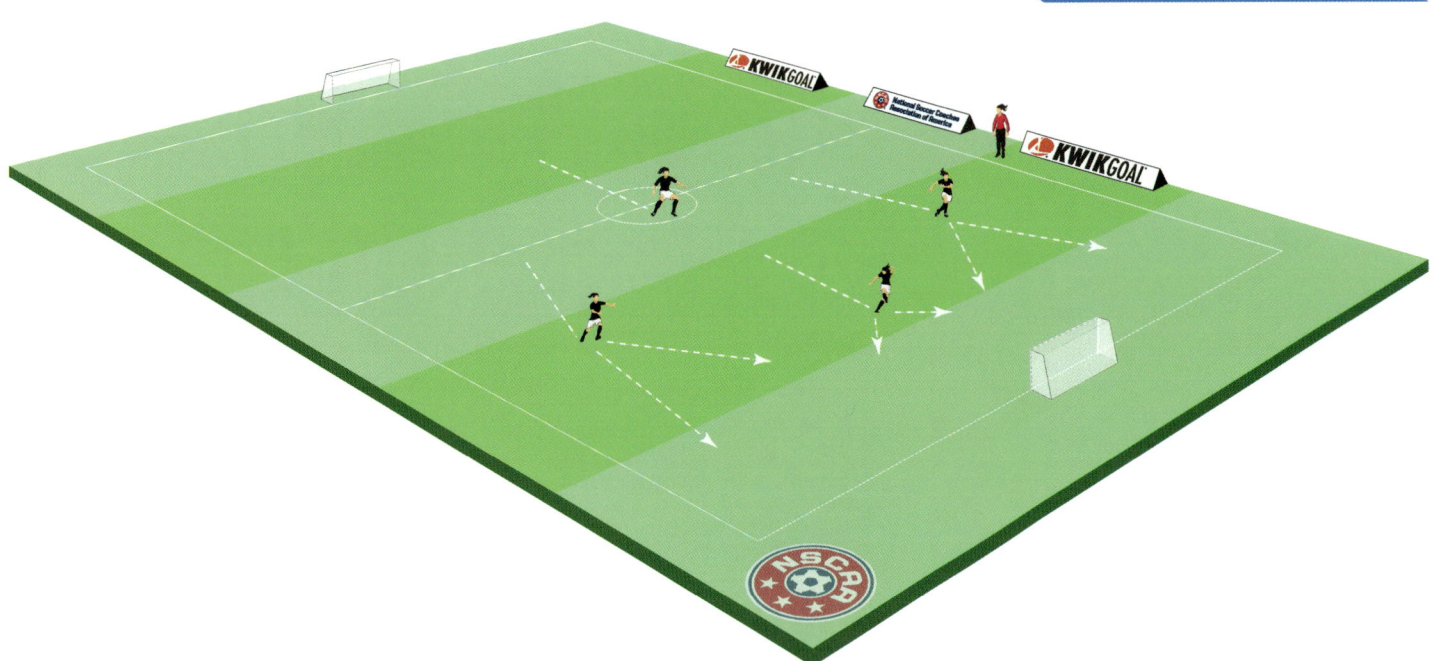

Features of this shape:
The central defender anchors the defense.
Left and right midfield players provide width and take up attacking positions behind and in advance of the striker in wide positions.
The striker remains central and provides team with length.

Defending Shape

Features of this shape:
Central defender drops deep to reduce the space between the back line and the goal.
Left and right midfield players drop back towards the goal and provide cover in front of the central defender, behind the striker and in wide positions.
The striker drops to provide cover in front of the central defender.

4v4 FORMATIONS - 0-2-2

Attacking Shape

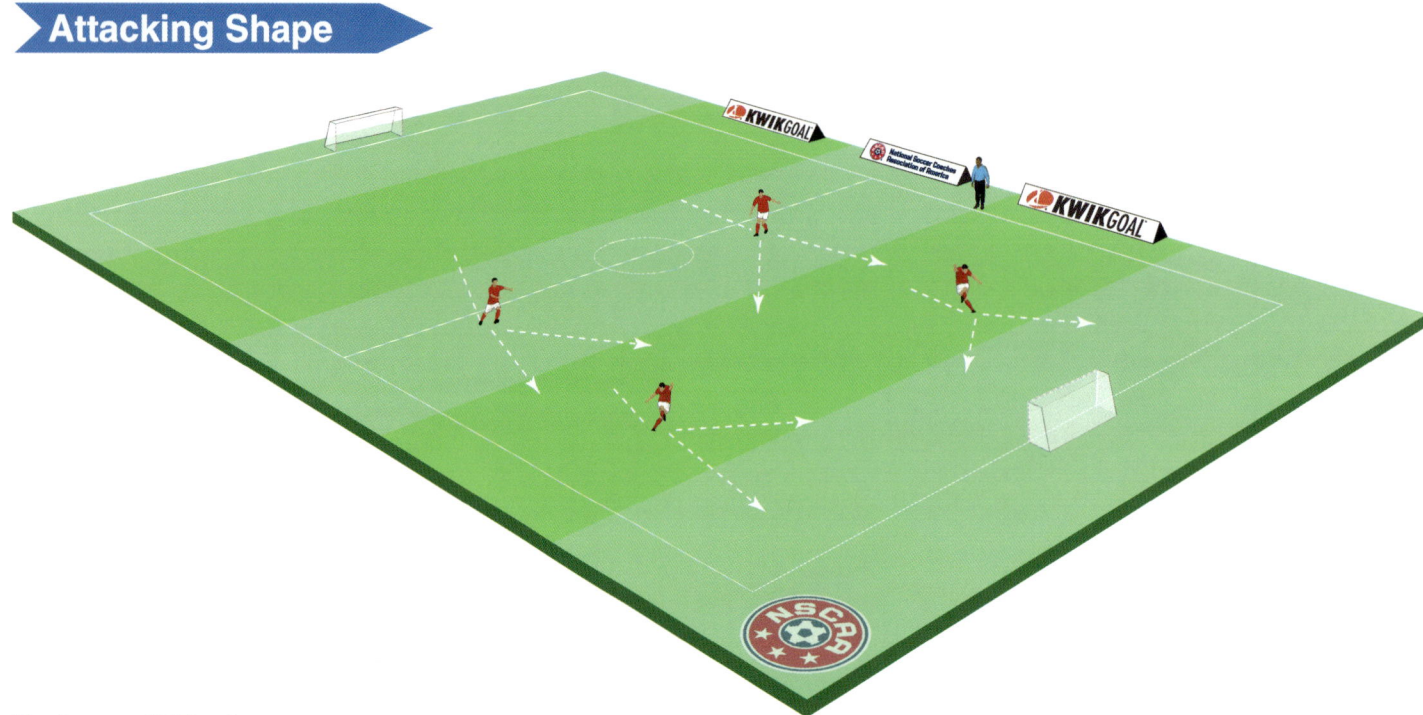

Features of this shape:
Players form an expanded box.
Left and right defenders move laterally - if the right defender moves wide the left defender 'tucks' in centrally.
On occasion the left or right defender may overlap wide.
The two strikers provide attacking length and work together - sliding across the field to support their partner.

Defending Shape

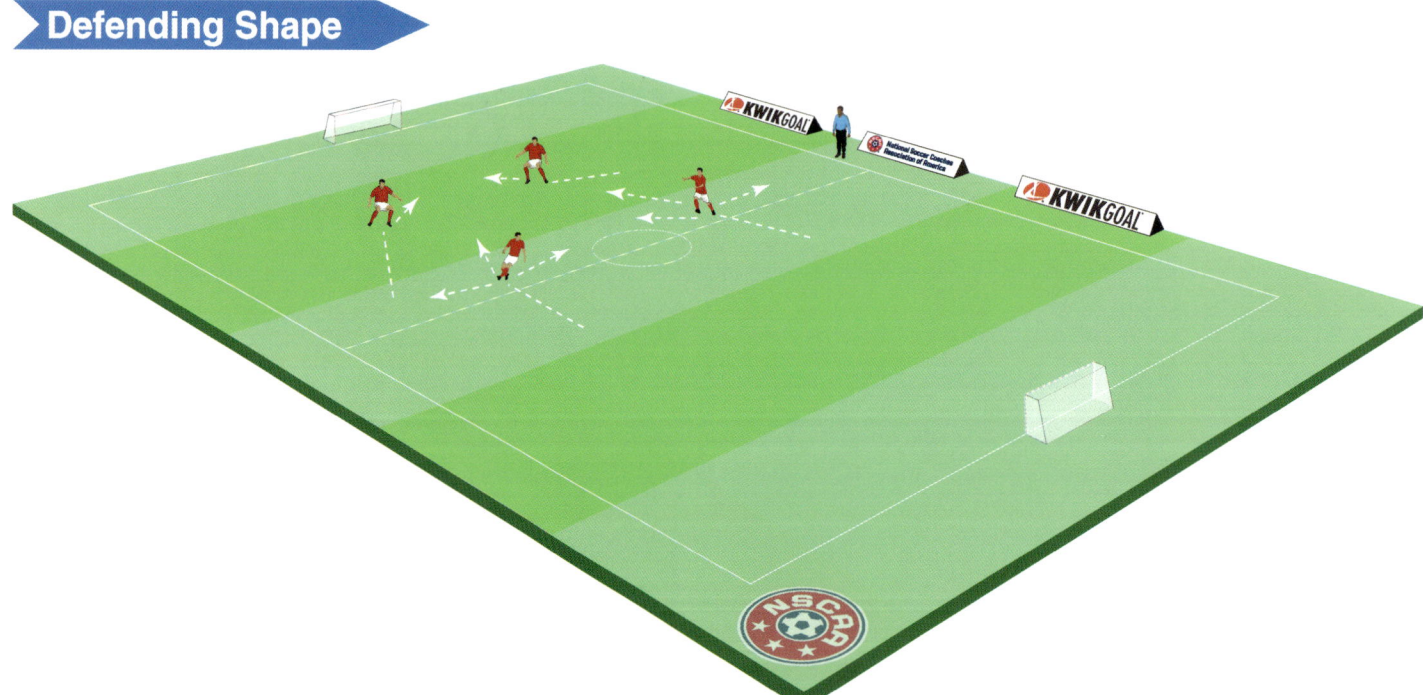

Features of this shape:
The left and right defenders drop deep and narrow to reduce the space between the back line and the goal.
In this formation there should be less room for the attacking team to play behind the defenders in wide positions.
Left and right strikers drop back towards the goal and provide cover in front of the defenders.
The strikers should attempt to 'double' team an attacker with the ball with their defensive partner.

4v4 FORMATIONS - 0-1-3

Attacking Shape

Features of this shape:
The most attacking formation of the 3 - with 3 players committed to the attack.
The wide attackers must make the field 'big' by maintaining the width.
The central defender must maintain his/her discipline and focus on defensive responsibilities.
The central striker should attempt to link up with the wide players and should penetrate behind the defense.

Defending Shape

Features of this shape:
Central defender drops deep to reduce the space between the back line and the goal. Player must delay attacks.
Left and right forwards must cover considerable ground and drop back towards the goal to provide cover and support for the central defender - the wide player on the weak side should tuck in centrally.
The striker drops to provide cover in front of the central defender..

WALL PASS FUNCTIONAL

Why use it?
This activity is a great way to work on combinations between attackers and midfield players and to introduce a wall pass. Teaching combination play in the final third is time well spent. Providing players options to beat an opponent 2v1 in different areas of the field allows for success and overall enjoyment. Doing this at a young age helps to create a solid base knowledge to build upon.

Set up
The area is half a 4v4 field - 15x20 yards. An appropriate size goal is at one end and the coach stands in the center with a large supply of balls. A defender starts 5 yards from goal and pairs of attackers stand either side of the coach on the halfway line.

How to play
The coach starts each sequence with a pass to either attacker. The attackers play 2v1 against the defender and attempts to score in the goal. The defender earns a point by winning possession and passing the ball to the coach. The coach can keep the same defender for 5-6 sequences, or the attacker receiving the pass from the coach becomes the next defender.

Coaching notes
Coaching Objectives: Teach midfield and attacking players to recognize when a wall pass is available and how to execute the combination. Players will learn visual and spatial cues that indicate that a wall pass is an option. For example, if the defender drops back towards the goal the receiver should dribble at pace. If the defender applies pressure to the ball carrier close to the halfway line a pass is likely the best option.
Coaching Tips: The coach can adjust the speed of attack and establish different starting points when serving the balls.

How to modify
Less Challenging: Encourage your defender to be overly aggressive. An overly aggressive defender will create more space for the attackers to perform a wall pass around and behind the defender. Patient or low pressure defending will make it hard to recognize the times when a wall pass is on. The coach can also start the activity without a defender.
More Challenging: Add a second defender to make teams even 2v2. This adjustment will result in less space and time for the attackers. Dribbling at the first defender and timing the wall pass will become even more important. If the activity becomes too challenging, consider starting one of the defenders behind the goal to provide more time for the attack to build up steam.

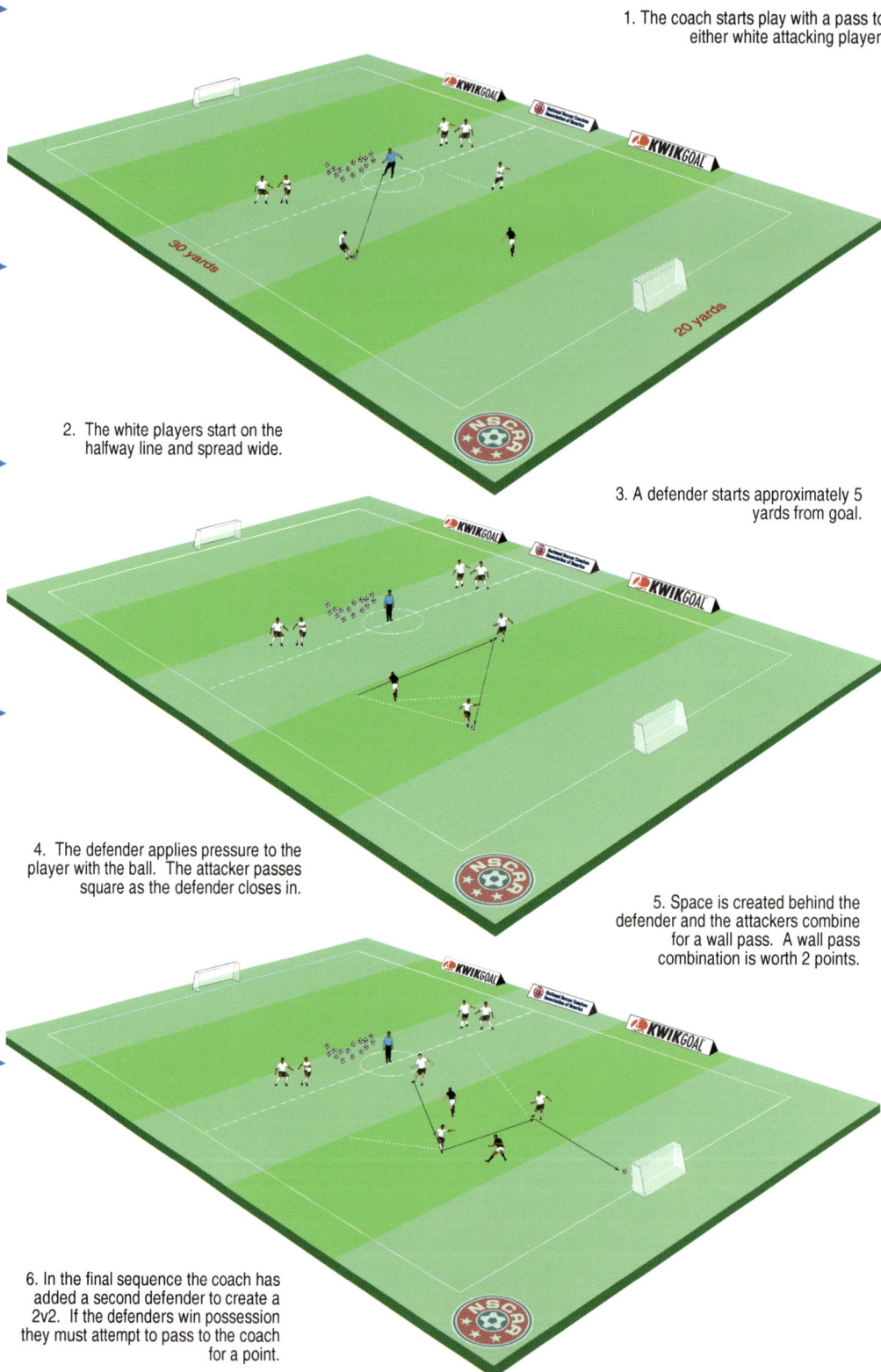

1. The coach starts play with a pass to either white attacking player.
2. The white players start on the halfway line and spread wide.
3. A defender starts approximately 5 yards from goal.
4. The defender applies pressure to the player with the ball. The attacker passes square as the defender closes in.
5. Space is created behind the defender and the attackers combine for a wall pass. A wall pass combination is worth 2 points.
6. In the final sequence the coach has added a second defender to create a 2v2. If the defenders win possession they must attempt to pass to the coach for a point.

Stage/s of development covered by activity
Stages 2 & 3 - 6-11 year old players.

Development themes and competencies
Top 3 Themes: Passing over short distances, passing combinations and defending as an individual.
Top 3 Competencies: Passing, receiving and support with and without the ball.

WALL PASS PHASE OF PLAY

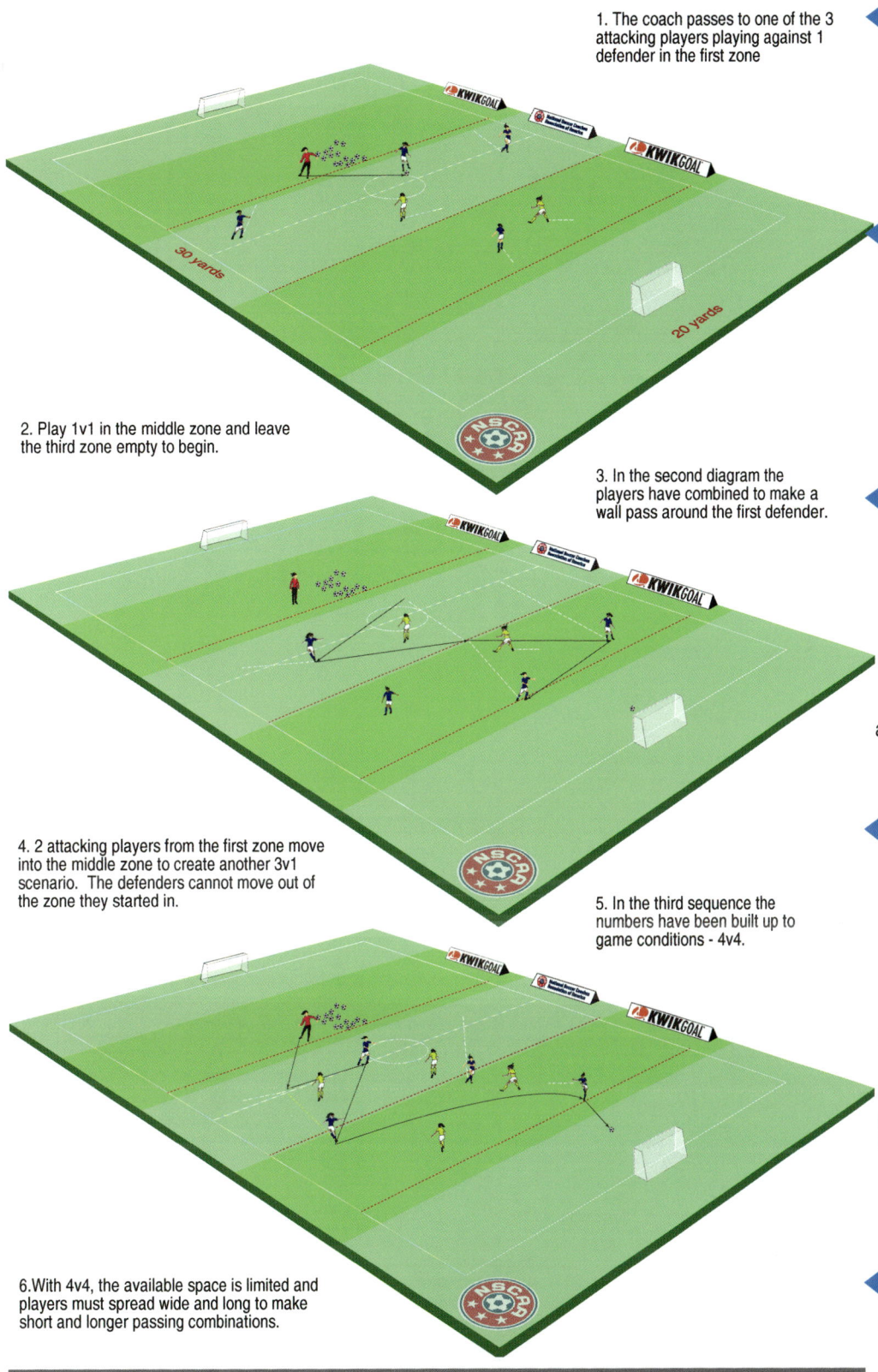

1. The coach passes to one of the 3 attacking players playing against 1 defender in the first zone

2. Play 1v1 in the middle zone and leave the third zone empty to begin.

3. In the second diagram the players have combined to make a wall pass around the first defender.

4. 2 attacking players from the first zone move into the middle zone to create another 3v1 scenario. The defenders cannot move out of the zone they started in.

5. In the third sequence the numbers have been built up to game conditions - 4v4.

6. With 4v4, the available space is limited and players must spread wide and long to make short and longer passing combinations.

Why use it?

This session progresses a simple technical wall-pass activity using all 4 attacking players. For younger age groups, staying connected as a team is important but difficult to achieve. This activity encourages midfield players to get forward to support and connect with the forward. The result should be more scoring opportunities and more players involved.

Set up

Two thirds of a 4v4 field is used and lines/cones denote 3 equal zones. An appropriate size goal is at one end of the field and the coach stands with the balls at the opposite end. Set up the attacking team in a 0-3-1 formation. In the zone furthest from goal play 3 attackers versus 1 defender and in the middle third 1v1. Initially the defenders are restricted to move in the zone in which they started.

How to play

The coach starts the game with a pass to one of the 3 attacking players in the zone closest to the coach. The attackers play 3v1 and attempt to advance the ball into the attacker standing in the middle zone. One of the defenders/midfield players can advance to the middle zone by dribbling or passing into the forward. This creates a 2v1 in the middle third. The final third remains empty until the attacking players either dribble or pass into the zone. The defending team scores a point by winning possession of the ball and passing to the coach.

Coaching notes

Coaching Objectives: Stress the importance of midfielders getting in the attack. Teaching midfielders to recognize visual and spatial cues that indicate when to go forward. Teach attacking players to recognize when a wall pass is available and to execute the combination. The support player may be the one on the opposite side of the field. It takes a lot of energy for the players to make support runs so plenty of encouragement and praise is needed.

Coaching Tips: Restricting movements of players to specific zones of the field allows the coach to create overload opportunities. In this activity the attackers have the advantage. In addition, preventing defenders from dropping into the final third provides the attackers with space behind the defense to make a wall pass.

How to modify

Less Challenging: Work on the pattern of play with passive defenders, or remove defenders entirely.

More Challenging: Add a second defender in the middle third and/or add a defender to the final third. Adding defenders minimizes space and consequently reduces time for the attackers. Less time and less space increases the importance of technical precision.

Stage/s of development covered by activity

Stages 2, 3 & 4 - 6-14 year old players.

Development themes and competencies

Top 3 Themes: Passing over short distances, passing combinations and defending as an individual.

Top 3 Competencies: Passing, receiving and support with and without the ball.

WALL PASS THE GAME

Why use it?
This activity progresses the passing theme into a 4v4 game played on a full field. To assist young players, the coach takes up strategic positions on the field during the flow of the game to help players better understand their roles. This methodology is called 'coaching in the game' and can be used quite effectively if the coach can stay out of the run of play.

Set up
This activity is played on a 4v4 field measuring 30x20 yards and two appropriate size goals are at each end. 2 teams of 4 players start in the coach's preferred formations, in this example both teams are set up in a diamond 0-1-2-1. Balls can be placed next to the goals and/or the halfway line so the coach can initiative a restart from the goal line.

How to play
Commence the game with a kick-off and let the players play for a few minutes uninterrupted so they get into the flow of the game. Instruct the players what commands will be used to stop the game and how you wish them to react. The coach may wish to remain on the sideline and enter the playing field with an announcement of "FREEZE". The player should stop immediately allowing the coach to recreate the previous sequence and then instruct and correct the play. The coach should seek to rehearse one good example before restarting the activity. It is important to use the game to draw out the main themes of the session, so the coach should seek opportunities to coach the wall pass. With young players in particular, the coach must expect players to forget the themes as they get engrossed in the game. To this end, be prepared to step in and demonstrate situations where a wall pass may be possible. Play for 10 minutes, take a break and go again.

Coaching notes
Coaching Objectives: Help players to recognize when a wall pass is available, timing of the pass and movement to support a teammate. Teach visual and spatial cues that tip off the dribbler and teammate when a wall pass is appropriate.
Coaching Tip: A good coaching strategy during a game-like activity is to speak with players when there is a natural stoppage in the game, such as a goal kick, throw in or free kick. Keeping the game flowing and avoiding too many interruptions will be appreciated by the players.

How to modify
Less Challenging: To increase the likelihood of the attacking team achieving a wall pass combination the coach can remove 1-2 defenders to create an attacking overload. The coach can also restrict 2 players from each team to stay in the attacking half.
More Challenging: Place a time restriction on the attacking team to get the ball forward and/or add 2-3 touch restrictions for each player.

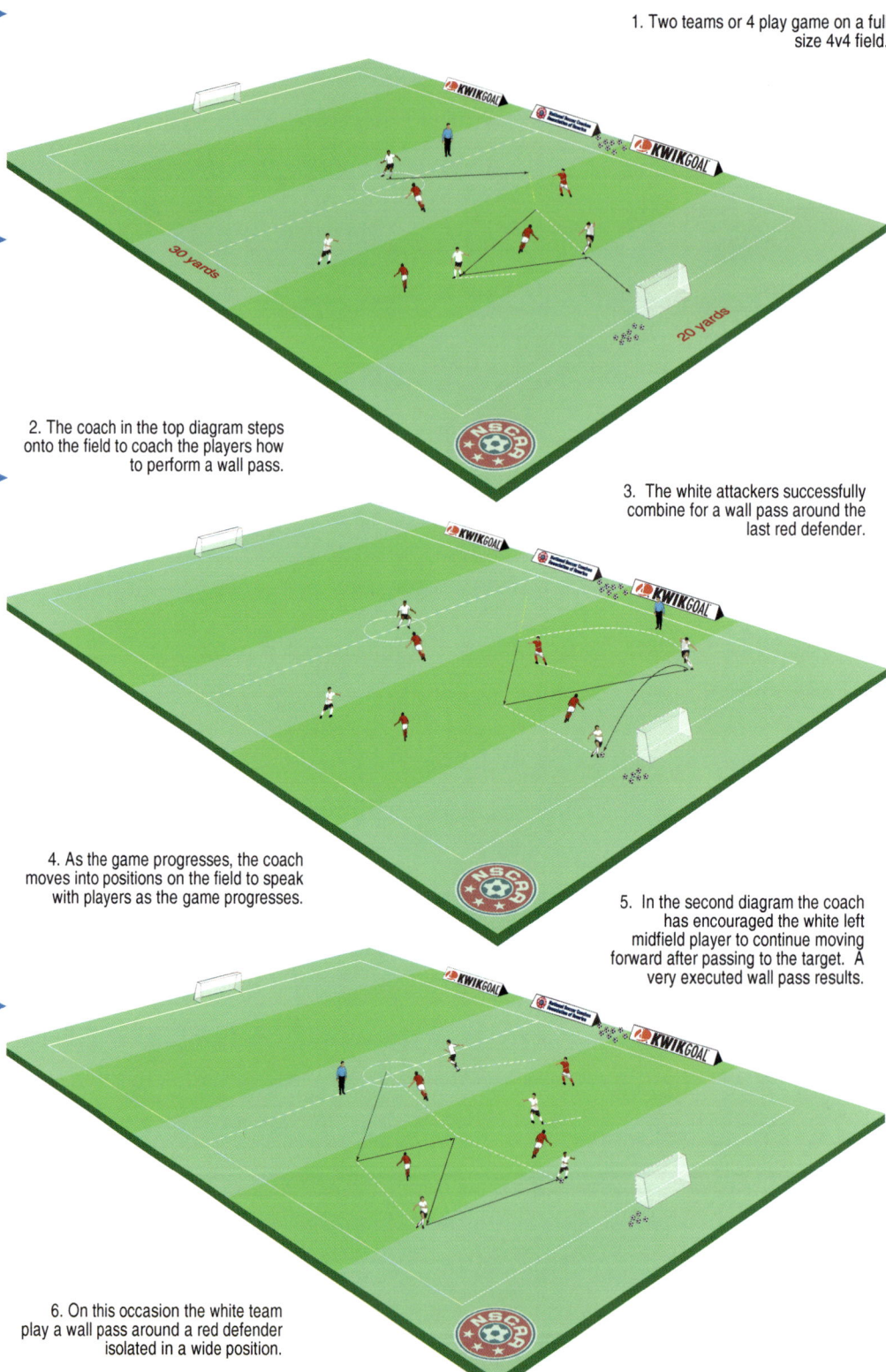

1. Two teams or 4 play game on a full size 4v4 field.
2. The coach in the top diagram steps onto the field to coach the players how to perform a wall pass.
3. The white attackers successfully combine for a wall pass around the last red defender.
4. As the game progresses, the coach moves into positions on the field to speak with players as the game progresses.
5. In the second diagram the coach has encouraged the white left midfield player to continue moving forward after passing to the target. A very executed wall pass results.
6. On this occasion the white team play a wall pass around a red defender isolated in a wide position.

Stage/s of development covered by activity
Stages 2, 3 and 4 - 6-14 year old players.

Development themes and competencies
Top 3 Themes: Passing over short distances, passing combinations and defending as unit.
Top 3 Competencies: Passing, receiving and support with and without the ball.

PRESSURE & COVER DEFENDING FUNCTIONAL

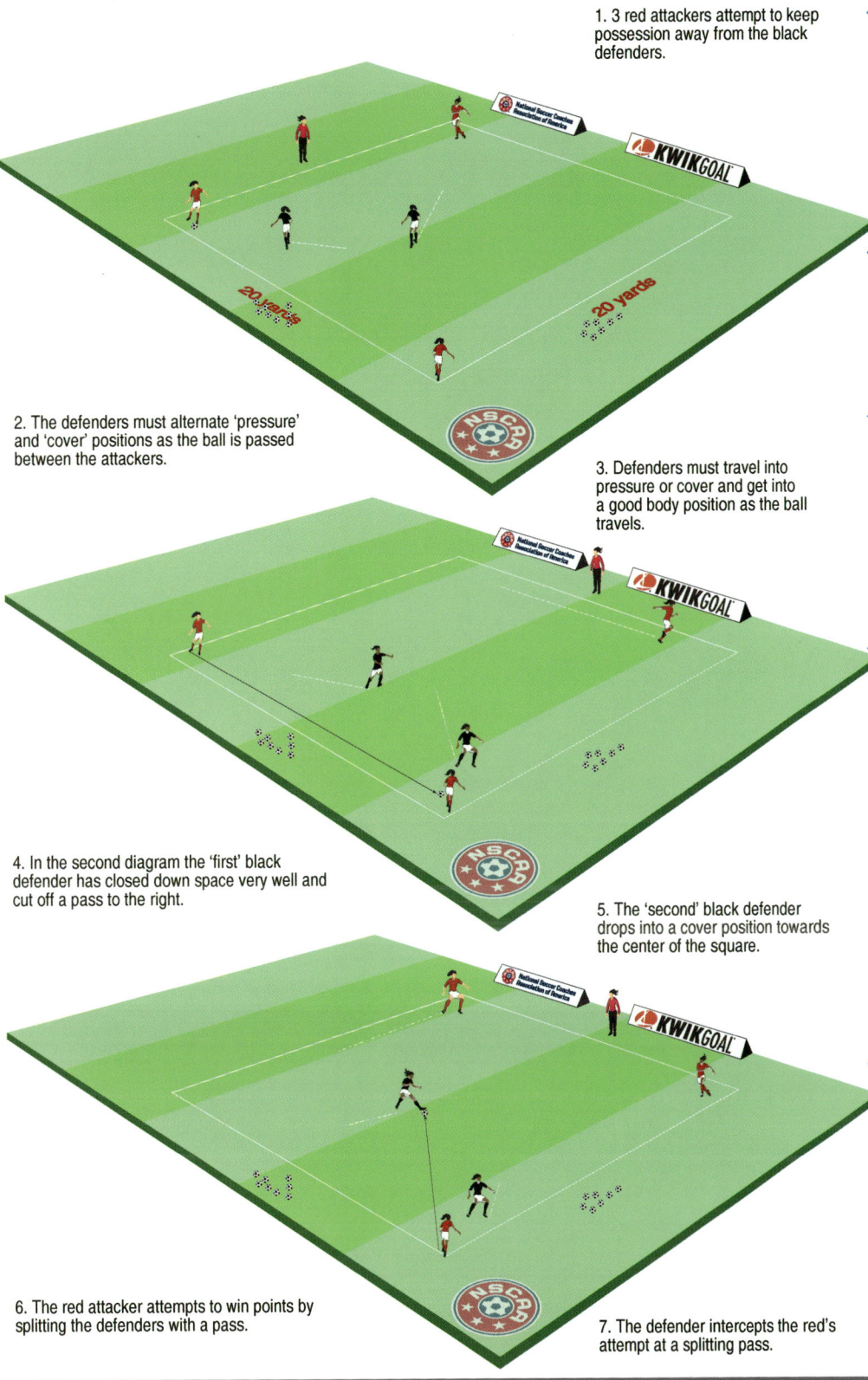

1. 3 red attackers attempt to keep possession away from the black defenders.

2. The defenders must alternate 'pressure' and 'cover' positions as the ball is passed between the attackers.

3. Defenders must travel into pressure or cover and get into a good body position as the ball travels.

4. In the second diagram the 'first' black defender has closed down space very well and cut off a pass to the right.

5. The 'second' black defender drops into a cover position towards the center of the square.

6. The red attacker attempts to win points by splitting the defenders with a pass.

7. The defender intercepts the red's attempt at a splitting pass.

Why use it?
This activity introduces players to the role of the first and second defenders - pressure and cover. It also demonstrates clearly what it looks like when two defenders 'get split'. It will help the defenders to understand the importance of communication, angle of the approach and body positioning.

Set up
The area is a 20x20 yards square with balls conveniently located outside the area. The coach can move around the edge of the area to coach individuals.

How to play
3 attackers stand in three corners of the area and 2 defenders are in the middle of the area. Attackers pass the ball to each other trying not to let the two defenders steal it; ultimately trying to 'split' the defenders down the middle with a pass. After 2 minutes change the defenders.

Coaching notes
Coaching Objectives: Defenders must communicate. The closest defender (1st) says 'BALL', and 2nd defender says 'COVER'. They move so they don't get 'split'. The covering defender must adjust distance and body angle depending on 1st defenders positioning.
Coaching Tips: One way the coach can keep the game moving and reduce the number of stoppages for changeovers is to have the defender hold a training vest. Once the defender has intercepted the ball or the attackers have lost possession, the defender drops the vest and exchanges positions with the offending attacker.

How to modify
Less Challenging: Insist the attackers must wait for the defenders to get in a good position before passing. Force the attackers to take at least 2 touches before making a pass - giving the defenders more time to get into a good defensive position.
More Challenging: Add an additional attacker to create a 4v4. Play in a circle - this condition will allow the attackers to move freely and harder for the defenders to visualize the split. Keep score for attackers v defenders – attackers get a point if they split the defense and defenders get a point if they steal the ball.

Stage/s of development covered by activity
Stages 2,3 & 4 - 6-14 year old players

Development themes and competencies
Top 3 Themes: Defending positioning - pressure and cover, 1v1/pairs defending and small group defending.
Top 3 Competencies: Defensive stance, applying defensive pressure and communication.

PRESSURE AND COVER DEFENDING PHASE

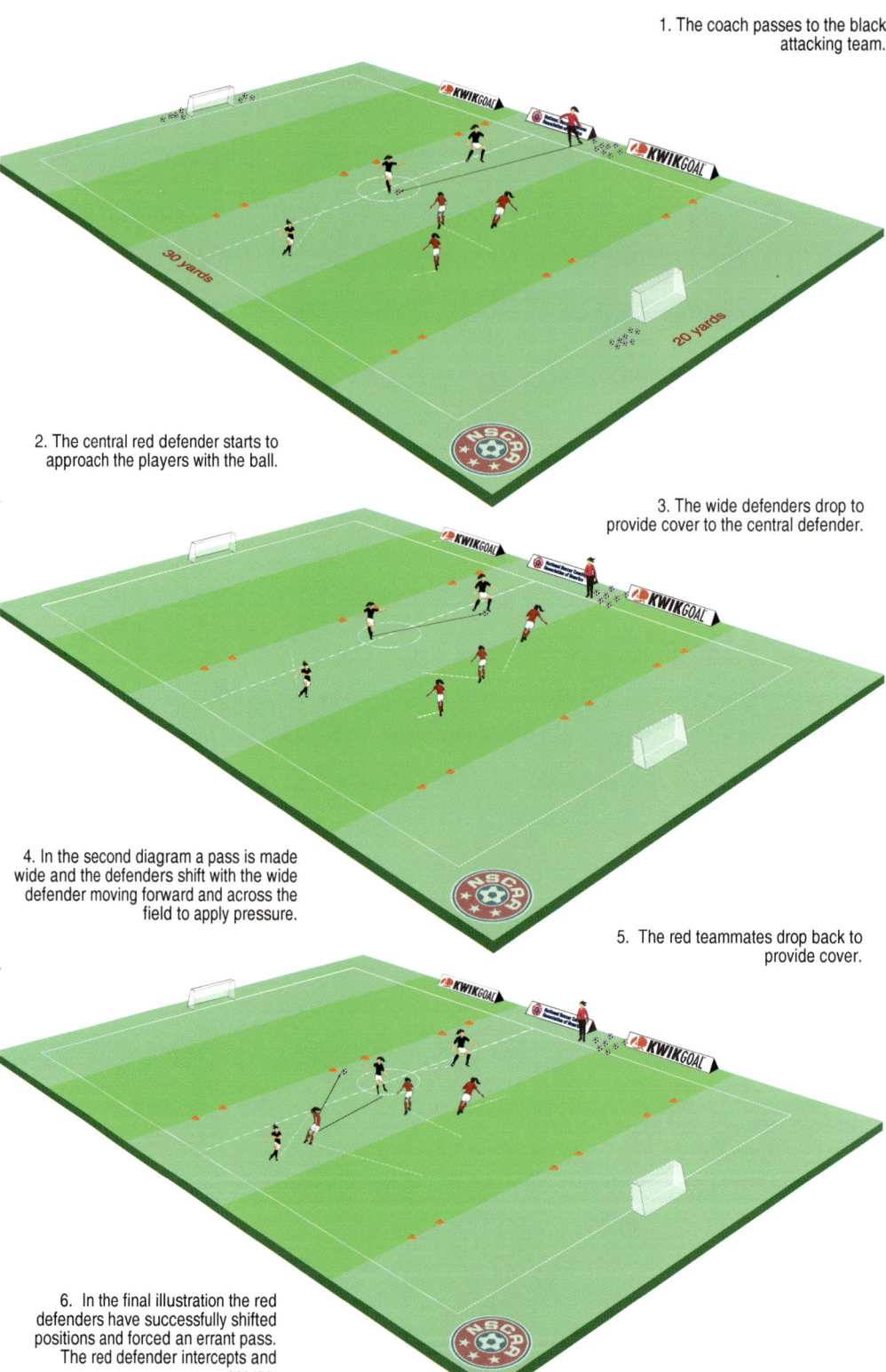

1. The coach passes to the black attacking team.
2. The central red defender starts to approach the players with the ball.
3. The wide defenders drop to provide cover to the central defender.
4. In the second diagram a pass is made wide and the defenders shift with the wide defender moving forward and across the field to apply pressure.
5. The red teammates drop back to provide cover.
6. In the final illustration the red defenders have successfully shifted positions and forced an errant pass. The red defender intercepts and scores.

Why use it?

Using multiple goals encourages the attacking team to switch the point of attack. Consequentially, the defenders are required to constantly adjust their defensive positioning to apply pressure and cover. The attacking players attempt to dribble and penetrate through the goal or recognize when to change direction with a pass.

Set up

This activity is played in the middle of a 4v4 field measuring 30x20 yards. The width of the field is 20 yards and the depth of the area 15 yards to create a rectangle. 3 goals are created across the width of the field for both teams to defend using cones approximately 2 yards apart. Both teams commence with 3 players and the coach stands on the side of the field with a large supply of balls.

How to play

The activity starts with a pass from the coach to either team. As the focus is on the defenders, the coach may wish to start with a 'pattern of play' - the central attacker passes the ball side to side to the wide players. The attackers do not attempt to penetrate at first and the defenders do not attempt to win the ball. Instead, as the ball is passed to the wide attacker the defenders move into pressure and cover positions. The coach can insist on the receiver 'holding' the ball for 2-3 seconds to allow the defenders to move into the correct positions. Once the coach is happy both teams understand their defensive roles, the game goes live. The attacking objective is to score in any of the 3 goals with a dribble or ground pass. The defenders attempt to win possession and attack the opponents goals. Restarts are from the coach.

Coaching notes

Coaching Objectives: The coach must work with the 3 defenders to create correct defensive shape - pressure and cover. When the ball is central the middle defender applies pressure and the wide defenders drop into a cover position. Cover defenders should be able to challenge an attacker if the pressure defender is beaten. When the ball is wide, the nearest defender applies pressure, the central players drop into cover and the furthest defender also drops deeper.

How to modify

Coaching Tip: Using multiple goals enable the coach to create multiple points of attack. This strategy is great for teaching young defenders how to move as a defensive unit.
Less Challenging: Start the activity with patterns of play and/or passive defending. Require attackers to play 3 touches minimum to slow down the play and allow defenders to adjust.
More challenging: Transition to free play. Add an extra attacker to the field to provide the defenders with more challenge.

Stage/s of development covered by activity

Stages 2, 3 and 4 - 6-14 year old players.

Development themes and competencies

Top 3 Themes: Defending positioning - pressure and cover, Defending as an individual, in pairs and small groups.
Top 3 Competencies: Defensive stance, applying defensive pressure and communication.

PRESSURE AND COVER DEFENDING GAME

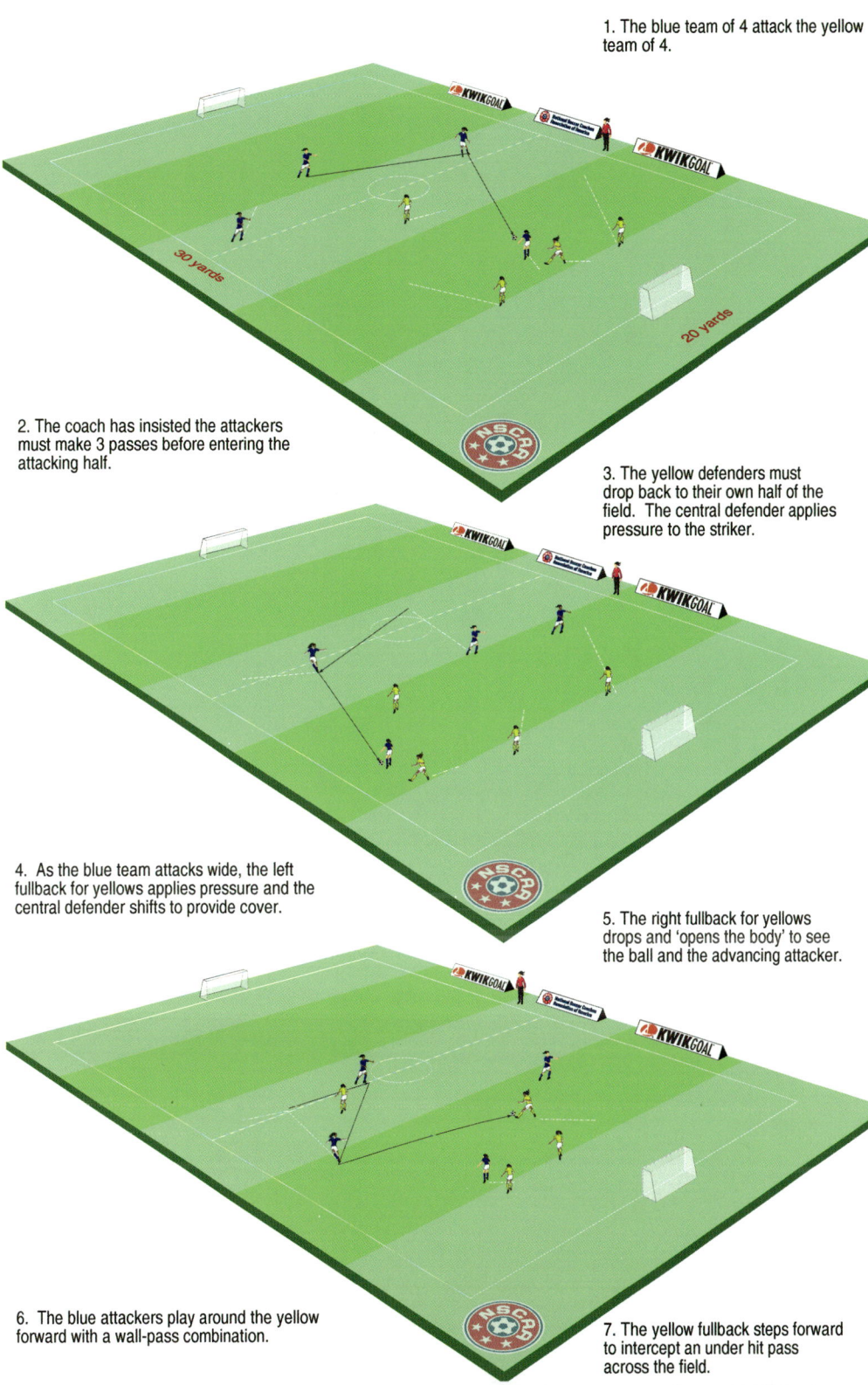

1. The blue team of 4 attack the yellow team of 4.

2. The coach has insisted the attackers must make 3 passes before entering the attacking half.

3. The yellow defenders must drop back to their own half of the field. The central defender applies pressure to the striker.

4. As the blue team attacks wide, the left fullback for yellows applies pressure and the central defender shifts to provide cover.

5. The right fullback for yellows drops and 'opens the body' to see the ball and the advancing attacker.

6. The blue attackers play around the yellow forward with a wall-pass combination.

7. The yellow fullback steps forward to intercept an under hit pass across the field.

Why use it?

It is paramount for defenders and midfielders to know how to apply pressure and cover. Reacting the visual cues is important. Employing 'coaching in the game' methodology allows the coach to provide timely advice and guidance for the players. The coach is able to show real game situations and tie them to topics and activities from previous practices.

Set up

This activity is played on a 4v4 field measuring 30x20 yards and two appropriate size goals are at each end. 2 teams of 4 players start in the coach's preferred formations. In this example the blue team is set up in a diamond 0-1-2-1 and the yellow team in 0-3-1. Balls can be placed next to the goals and/or the halfway line so the coach can initiative a restart from the goal line.

How to play

Play a full complement of players for both teams - 4v4. Players are instructed the coach will stop the flow of play a few times to make a point or correction based on the topic. The coach will remain on the sideline and will enter the playing field with an announcement of "FREEZE", and with the players frozen the coach will make the coaching point. Play normal rules and seek opportunities to reinforce the roles of pressure and cover defenders.

Coaching notes

Coaching Objectives: Help players to recognize the visual cues to shift defensive positions and know who is the first (pressure) defender and who are the 2nd and 3rd defenders. Demonstrate the importance of collective defending in the defensive third. Stress the importance of all 4 players getting into good defensive positions..
Coaching Tips: Pressure should be applied as quickly as possible and this is often done while the ball is in flight. Assist players to move as the ball is travelling and not wait for the ball to arrive before moving. Often, timely movement by the defenders will place the receiver under sufficient pressure to force a turnover.

How to modify

Less Challenging: Require an attacking player or two to remain in their half of the field when transitioning to the attack. This condition will give the defenders more time and less space to cover. A similar result can be achieved by insisting the defending team retreats to defend from halfway, or the attacking team must pass back to the central defender before advancing forward.
More Challenging: As the ball transitions, reduce the number of defenders to 3, with the player furthest forward dropping off the field. Alternatively, speed up the attack by giving the attacking team 5 seconds to score.

Stage/s of development covered by activity

Stages 2, 3 and 4 - 6-14 year old players.

Development themes and competencies

Top 3 Themes: Defending positioning - pressure and cover, defending as an individual, in pairs and small groups.
Top 3 Competencies: Defensive stance, applying defensive pressure and communication.

ATTACKING WITH WIDTH FUNCTIONAL

Why use it?

Establishing field awareness and options for attackers is important in solving the games evolving situations. This activity gives the players numerous patterns and the coach plenty of opportunities to work with players on support movement. The wide players need to be aware of the timing of their runs forward.

Set up

The set up is a 20x20 yard square with a 4 yard end zone stretching the width of the area at each end. The coach stands at outside one end of the area with a large supply of balls. Only the attacking players are allowed to enter the end zone closest to the coach. There are 3 attackers and 2 defenders to start the activity.

How to play

The attacking objective is for the 3 players to pass the 2 defenders and stop the ball in the opponent's end zone. With a numerical advantage the attacking team should attempt to play around the 2 defenders. To achieve this objective one player should start in a central position and the other two players stretch the attack by getting as wide as possible. The coach always starts with the ball and plays to the central attacker, who must decide to either pass to a teammate or dribble towards the opponents end zone. If a defender applies pressure to the central attacker there will be at least one wide player available to pass to. If the defenders drop back or split to mark the wide players the central player can dribble. Each time the attackers are able to stop the ball in the end zone they win a point. If the defenders win possession they must play a pass to the coach for a point.

Coaching notes

Coaching Objectives: The coach can teach the players various options to penetrate space behind a defense, such as, dribbling, passing around the side of the defenders and passing between defenders. The coach can also impress upon the players the need to maintain good team attacking shape and spacing. The players will have to decide whether to penetrate or switch the point of attack.
Coaching Tip: In a relatively straight forward activity the coach can allow players some time to attempt different solutions to the challenge. If players struggle to find solutions, offer some options and patterns and allow the players more attempts.

How to modify

Less Challenging: Reduce the number of defenders. With less pressure on the ball, the attacking team should have more success in moving the ball and into the end zone.
More Challenging: Add a third defender. This will make the activity more game like and will increase the pressure on the attacking team. Restrict the number of touches to two. This will make the attacking team pass the ball and emphasize the importance of the first touch being positive and purposeful.

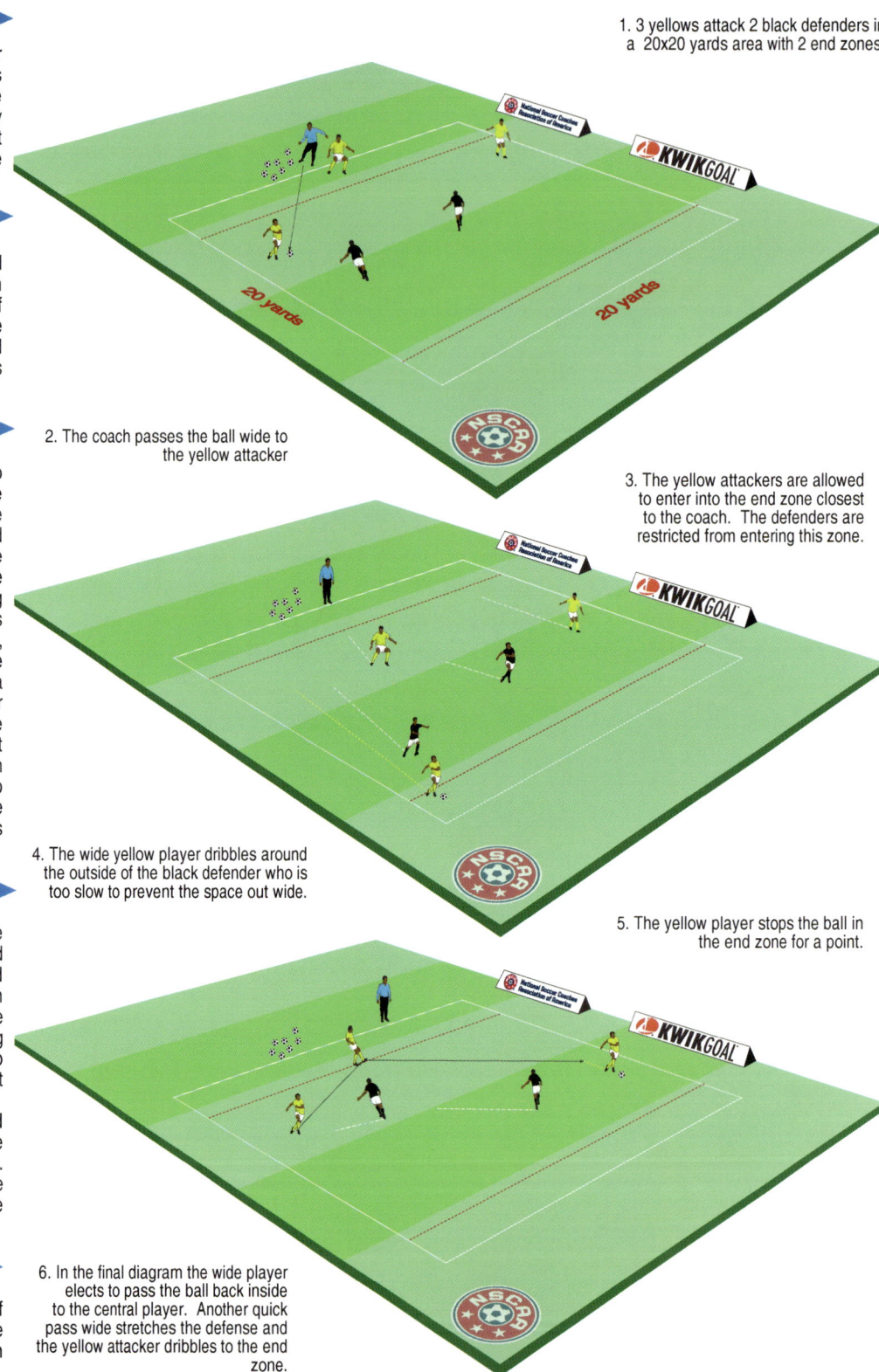

1. 3 yellows attack 2 black defenders in a 20x20 yards area with 2 end zones.

2. The coach passes the ball wide to the yellow attacker

3. The yellow attackers are allowed to enter into the end zone closest to the coach. The defenders are restricted from entering this zone.

4. The wide yellow player dribbles around the outside of the black defender who is too slow to prevent the space out wide.

5. The yellow player stops the ball in the end zone for a point.

6. In the final diagram the wide player elects to pass the ball back inside to the central player. Another quick pass wide stretches the defense and the yellow attacker dribbles to the end zone.

Stage/s of development covered by activity

Stages 2, 3 and 4 - 6-14 year old players.

Development themes and competencies

Top 3 Themes: Dribbling, passing over a short distance and creating space.
Top 3 Competencies: Passing and receiving, movement off the ball and providing width in support of the ball carrier.

ATTACKING WITH WIDTH PHASE

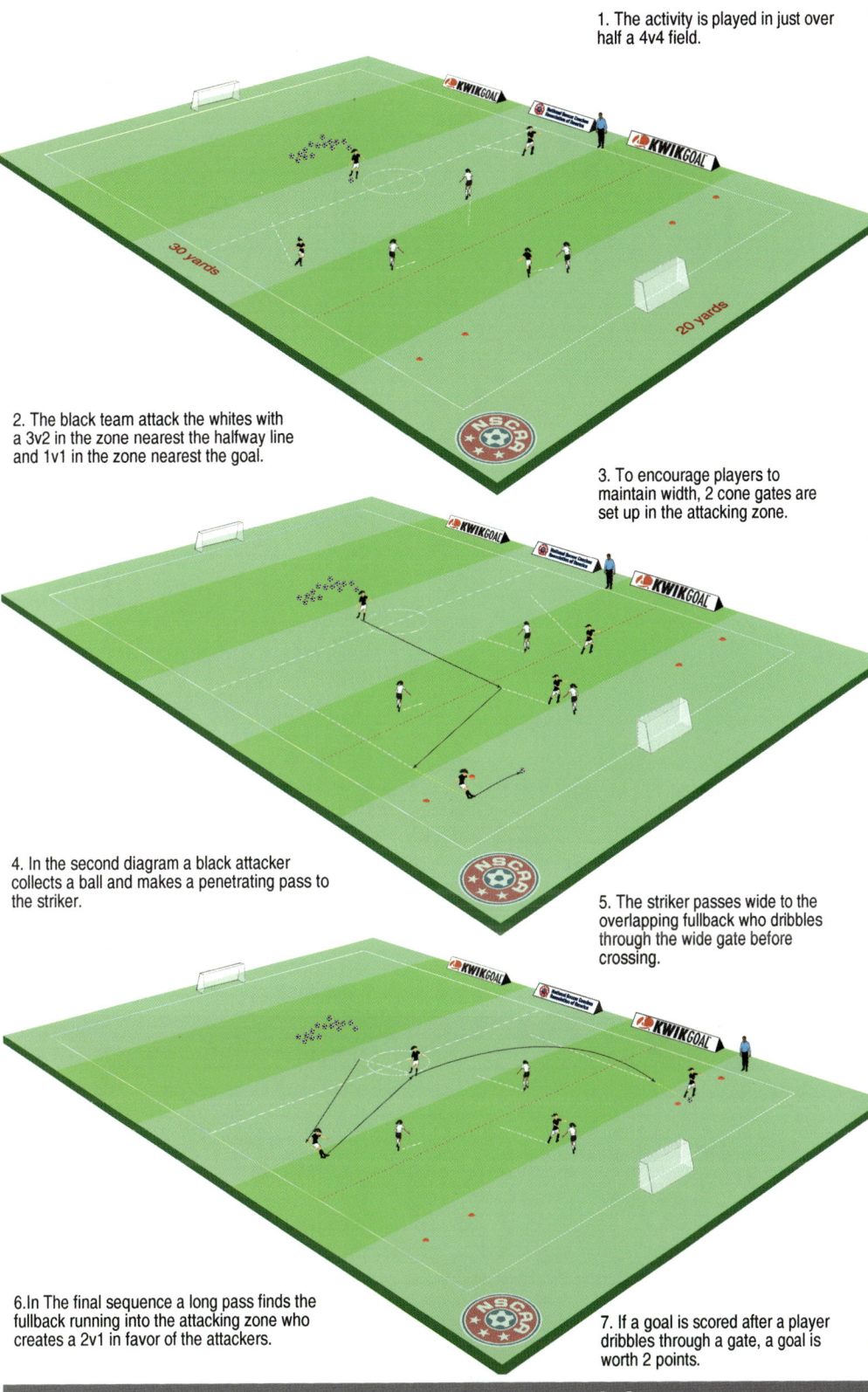

1. The activity is played in just over half a 4v4 field.

2. The black team attack the whites with a 3v2 in the zone nearest the halfway line and 1v1 in the zone nearest the goal.

3. To encourage players to maintain width, 2 cone gates are set up in the attacking zone.

4. In the second diagram a black attacker collects a ball and makes a penetrating pass to the striker.

5. The striker passes wide to the overlapping fullback who dribbles through the wide gate before crossing.

6. In The final sequence a long pass finds the fullback running into the attacking zone who creates a 2v1 in favor of the attackers.

7. If a goal is scored after a player dribbles through a gate, a goal is worth 2 points.

Why use it?
Excellent activity for training the wide players in the attack. This activity gives players many different patterns for attacking from the flanks in combination with the midfield and forward players. All 4 players are involved and the action occurs in the attacking half of the field.

Set up
This activity is played in just over half a 4v4 field measuring 20x20 yards. An appropriate size goal is at one end. Two zones split the field. Start with 4 attackers against 3 defenders, with a 3v2 in the zone closest to halfway and 1v1 in the zone closest to the goal. In the attacking end zone, place two 2 yards wide gates approximately 3 yards off the end line. A large supply of balls are situated 5 yards over the halfway line.

How to play
The attacking objective is score in the goal by building up play for the defense/midfield to the forward and create an overload of attackers in the attacking zone. The play commences with an attacker collecting a ball from the pile and dribbling across halfway. Once the attacker dribbles across the halfway line the game is live and the 2 defenders can attempt to win the ball. With a 3v2 numerical advantage the attackers should attempt to play around the defenders or pass into the forward. The defenders are restricted from leaving their assigned area, but the attackers can move freely. The attackers should attempt to overload the last defender and score in the goal. To encourage the attackers to maintain the width, a goal scored after a player dribbles through a wide gate is worth two points. If the defenders win possession they must dribble across the halfway line for a point.

Coaching notes
Coaching Objectives: Quick ball movement should result in the attackers exploiting the numerical advantage in each area. Keeping the width stretches the defenders and creates more attacking space.
Coaching Tips: Adding the wide gates offers an additional incentive for the wide players to remain wide.

How to modify
Less Challenging: Start with 1 defender in the midfield zone. By reducing the number of defenders in the first zone, the attacking team will have more success moving the ball forward.
More Challenging: Add a second defender into the final zone.

Stage/s of development covered by activity
Stages 2, 3 and 4 - 6-14 year old players.

Development themes and competencies
Top 3 Themes: Dribbling, passing over a short distance and creating space.
Top 3 Competencies: Passing and receiving, movement off the ball and providing width in support of the ball carrier.

ATTACKING WITH WIDTH GAME

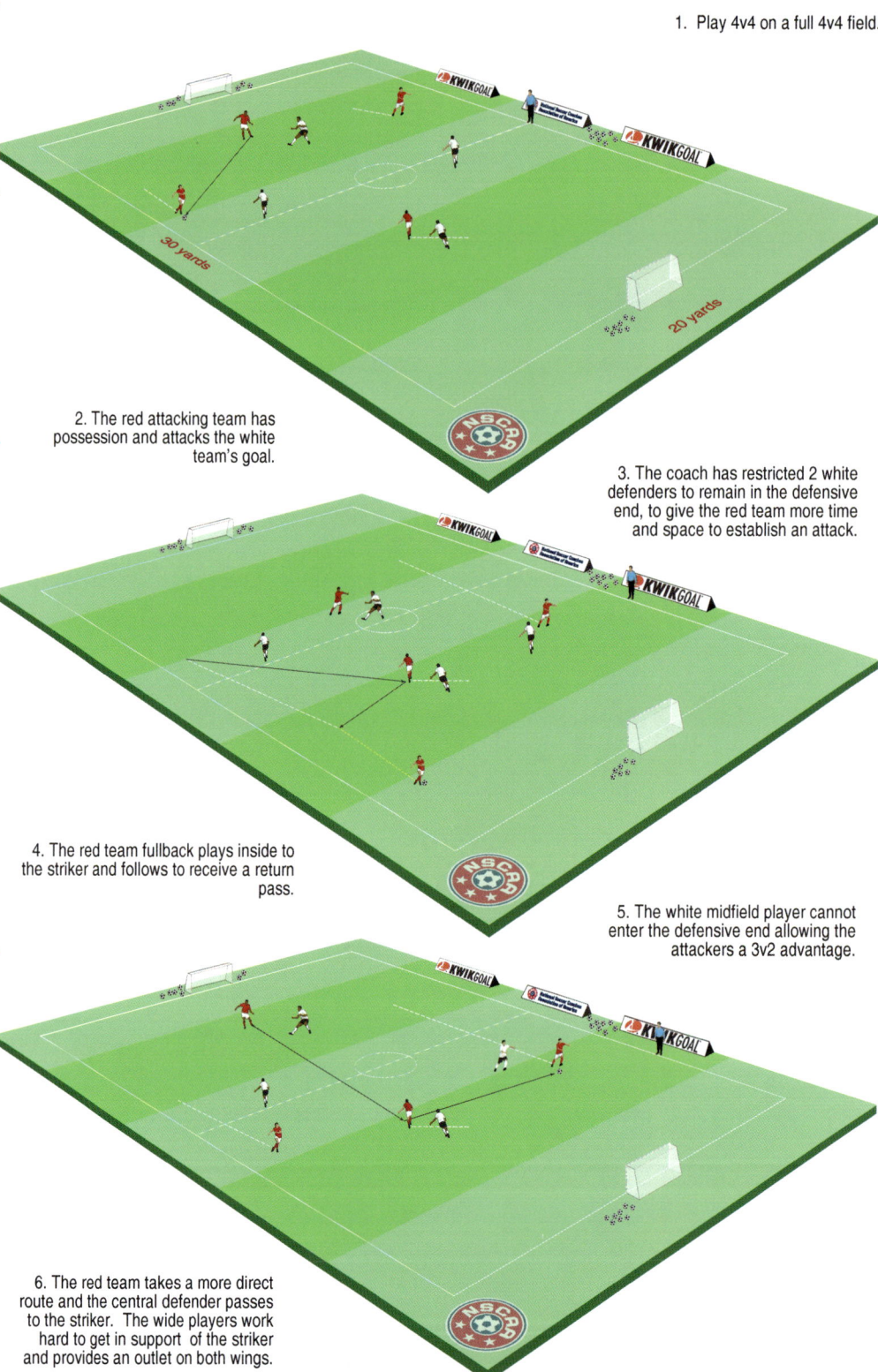

Why use it?
We now progress the theme of creating width in attack into a game-like environment. This activity would be ideal at the end of a session to complement a technical or functional session to teach players when and how to support in wide positions.

Set up
This activity is played on a 4v4 field measuring 30x20 yards and two appropriate size goals are at each end. 2 teams of 4 players start in the coach's preferred formations, in this example both teams are set up in a diamond 0-1-2-1. Balls can be placed next to the goals and/or the halfway line so the coach can initiate a restart from the goal line.

How to play
Play a full complement of players for both teams - 4v4. Players are instructed the coach will stop the flow of play a few times to make a point or correction based on the topic. The coach will remain on the sideline and will enter the playing field with an announcement of "FREEZE", and with the players frozen the coach will make the coaching point. Play normal rules. The attacking players to the left and right of the diamond should stay as wide as possible to 'stretch' the defense horizontally. This shape will create 'seams' between the defenders allowing space for a penetrating pass to the striker. If the defenders remain in a compact shape, the attackers exploit the width and play 'around' the defenders. During the game the coach can freeze the play, demonstrate a preferred sequence and then restart play.

Coaching notes
Coaching Objectives: The primary objective is for the attacking team to make the field as 'big' as possible by spreading wide and long. Creating space on the field typically favours the attackers.
Coaching Tip: Try to make stoppages to the game short and instruction concise. Ideally, the coach is able to identify a good example of a passing combination in wide areas to compliment and reinforce. If not, manufacture a sequence so the players can 'see' what you are looking for them to repeat.

How to modify
Less Challenging: To increase the likelihood of the attacking team achieving a wall pass combination, the coach can remove 1-2 defenders to create an attacking overload. The coach can also restrict 2 players from each team to stay in the attacking half.
More Challenging: Place a time restriction on the attacking team to get the ball forward and/or add 2-3 touch restrictions for each player.

1. Play 4v4 on a full 4v4 field.
2. The red attacking team has possession and attacks the white team's goal.
3. The coach has restricted 2 white defenders to remain in the defensive end, to give the red team more time and space to establish an attack.
4. The red team fullback plays inside to the striker and follows to receive a return pass.
5. The white midfield player cannot enter the defensive end allowing the attackers a 3v2 advantage.
6. The red team takes a more direct route and the central defender passes to the striker. The wide players work hard to get in support of the striker and provides an outlet on both wings.

Stage/s of development covered by activity
Stages 2, 3 and 4 - 6-14 year old players.

Development themes and competencies
Top 3 Themes: Dribbling, passing over a short distance and creating space.
Top 3 Competencies: Passing and receiving, movement off the ball and providing width in support of the ball carrier.

DEFENSIVE STOP WITH ATTACKING TRANSITION FUNCTIONAL

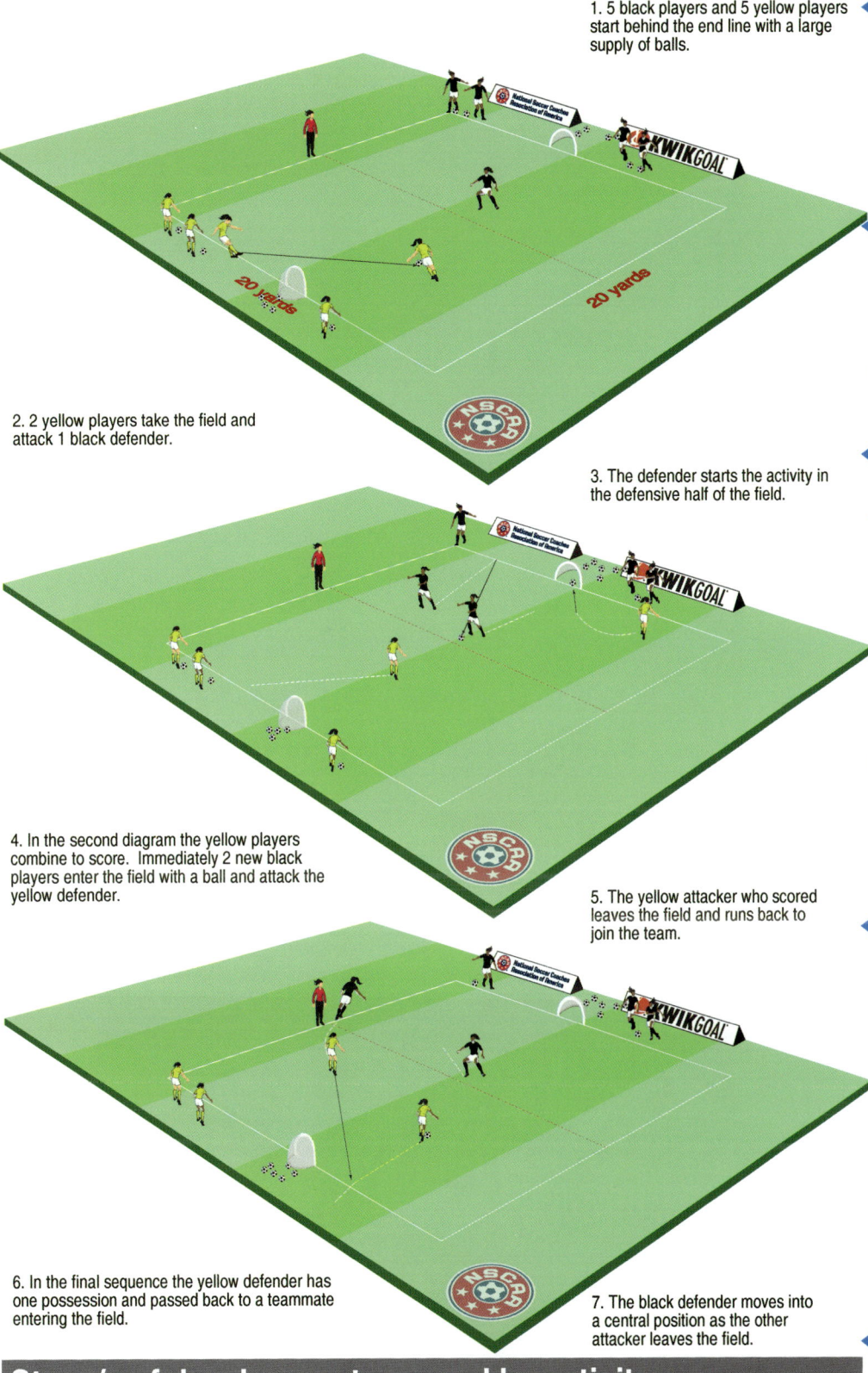

1. 5 black players and 5 yellow players start behind the end line with a large supply of balls.

2. 2 yellow players take the field and attack 1 black defender.

3. The defender starts the activity in the defensive half of the field.

4. In the second diagram the yellow players combine to score. Immediately 2 new black players enter the field with a ball and attack the yellow defender.

5. The yellow attacker who scored leaves the field and runs back to join the team.

6. In the final sequence the yellow defender has one possession and passed back to a teammate entering the field.

7. The black defender moves into a central position as the other attacker leaves the field.

Why use it?
This is fast paced and continuous activity creating a full game like environment. Focus on communication, distance and angles of the pressure defender. Working hard to win the ball back and then giving it right back to the other team is a common challenge for coaches. This activity raises the importance of keeping the ball after winning it.

Set up
The set up for this activity is a 20x20 yards area with 2 mini goals placed along 2 sides. A line of cones are used to split the field into 2 zones. 5 players start on each team and the coach stands on the sideline to view the action. Each team should collect and maintain a good supply of balls behind each goal to allow the game to flow continuously.

How to play
The focus of the activity is to work on individual defending, with particular emphasis on applying pressure to the ball carrier. 2 players from the attacking team start the game against 1 defender. The attackers must attempt to beat the defender and score in the mini goal. If the defender wins possession a new teammate joins the defender and an attacking player leaves the field to create a 2v1 in the opposite direction. If the defender manages to 'stop' the attack and retains possession of the ball, the defender must pass backwards to a teammate entering the field from the end line. A backwards pass provides time for one defender to retreat into a good position and the other player to leave the field. It also reinforces with the players that a pass does not always need to be played forward. If a goal is scored or the ball leaves the field, a new attacker joins from the end line dribbling or passing the ball.

Coaching notes
Coaching Objectives: In a transitional moment where the team has lost possession of the ball, the coach should help players to make good decisions and quickly assess the danger. In this activity the defender must be encouraged to run back into the defensive half of the field whilst facing the ball. Once the defender has minimized the risk from a long shot, the defender can then start to close down space and apply pressure on the ball.
Coaching Tips: It is important for the coach to manage different variables increasing the likelihood of success. In this situation the coach creates zones, enforces a back pass by the attackers and insists on the defender retreating to the defensive zone in an effort to highlight the main defensive theme.

How to modify
Less Challenging: Lengthen the field by 5-7 yards to give the defender more time to recover. If the defender is getting beaten regularly add a 2nd defender.
More Challenging: Lift the restriction of the back pass before commencing the attack. This change will speed up play and result in the defender having to move with greater urgency.

Stage/s of development covered by activity
Stages 2, 3 and 4 - 6-14 year old players.

Development themes and competencies
Top 3 Themes: Individual defending - pressure and patience, short passing and transition.
Top 3 Competencies: 1v1 defending, support and dribbling.

DEFENSIVE STOP WITH ATTACKING TRANSITION PHASE

Why use it?
In this phase of play activity we continue the theme of creating a defensive stop and transitioning into an immediate attack. The game is played on a modified 4v4 field with a full compliment of players on both teams.

Set up
This activity is played on a 4v4 field measuring 30x20 yards. An end zone is created at both ends of the field approximately 4 yards in depth and stretching the width of the field. A line of cones are placed 3 yards from each side line to narrow the field to begin the activity. The coach starts on the side line with a large supply of balls. One player from each team starts in an end zone and in the center play 3v3.

How to play
The coach starts play with a pass to either team in the center of the area. The attacking objective is to pass to the target player to score a point. The focus of this session is defending and both teams must attempt to win possession and transition with a counter attack to the other target player. Cones placed inside the sideline reduce the available space and consequently limit the amount of space the defenders have to cover. The defensive objective is to force a turnover of the ball by working on individual pressure and in pairs as 'pressure' and 'cover' defenders. As the defenders start to experience success, lift the cones to provide the attackers with more space.

Coaching notes
Coaching Objectives: When the defending team wins possession encourage the team losing possession to attempt to win the ball back. A pass back to the target player can alleviate pressure and provide the attacking team with controlled possession. Sometimes the players can pass directly to the target and in other situations the players can combine with another teammate before playing to the target. Coaching Tip: The quick transition from attack to defense necessitates clear communication between the defenders.

How to modify
Less Challenging: Do not play continuously. After an attempt to score by one team, stop the play and teams set up again, switching offensive and defensive roles. Slow down the passing by the attackers - add a minimum touch restriction. This will enable the defenders to move into position before having to move again. The coach could also make the width of activity smaller, creating compactness to benefit the defenders.
More Challenging: Limiting touches for the attackers will speed up the play, forcing defenders to think and move more quickly. The coach can also widen the field.

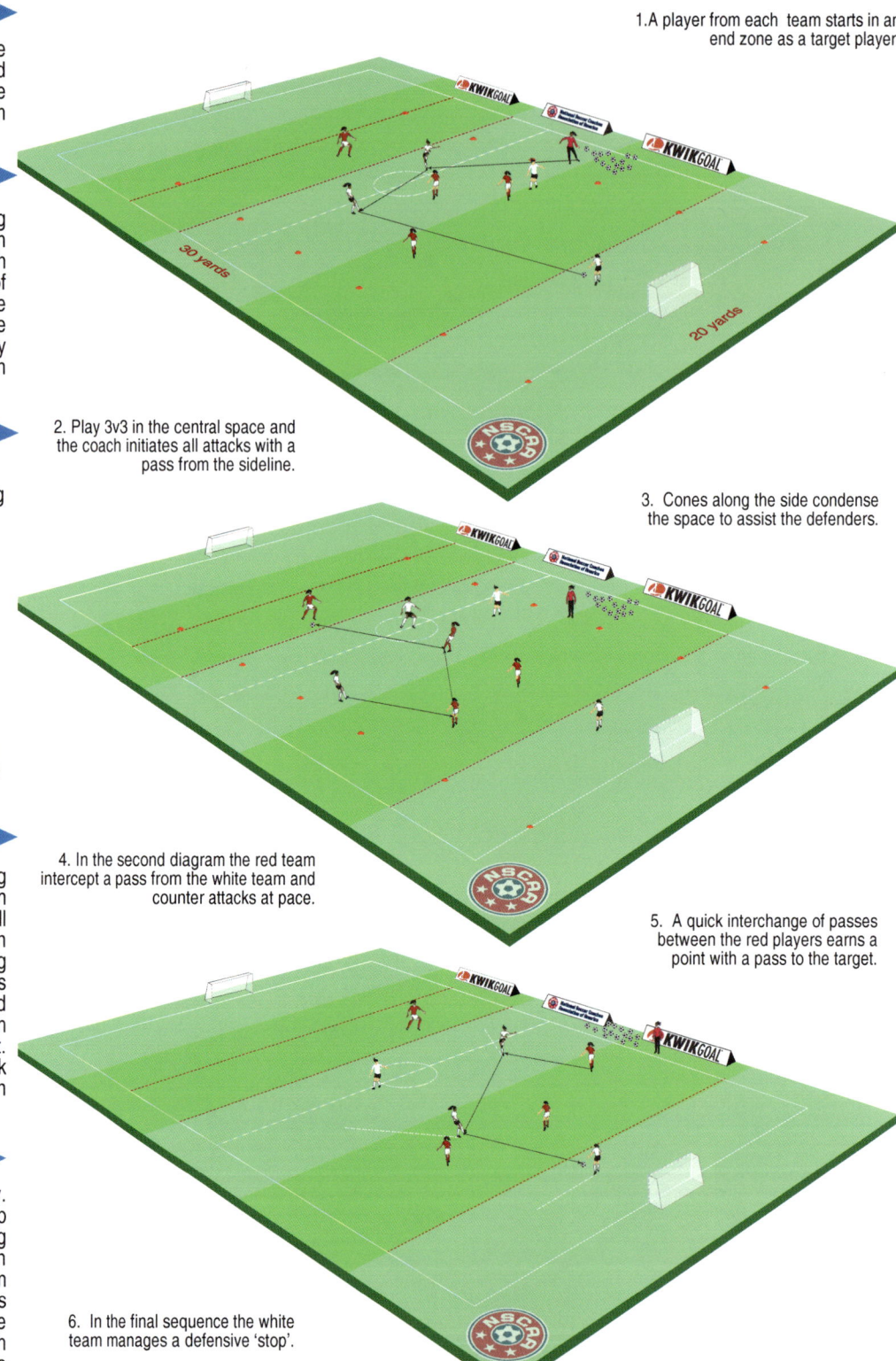

1. A player from each team starts in an end zone as a target player.

2. Play 3v3 in the central space and the coach initiates all attacks with a pass from the sideline.

3. Cones along the side condense the space to assist the defenders.

4. In the second diagram the red team intercept a pass from the white team and counter attacks at pace.

5. A quick interchange of passes between the red players earns a point with a pass to the target.

6. In the final sequence the white team manages a defensive 'stop'.

Stage/s of development covered by activity
Stages 2, 3 and 4 - 6-14 year old players.

Development themes and competencies
Top 3 Themes: Individual defending - pressure and patience, pairs defending - pressure/cover and transition.
Top 3 Competencies: 1v1 defending, support and dribbling.

DEFENSIVE STOP WITH ATTACKING TRANSITION GAME

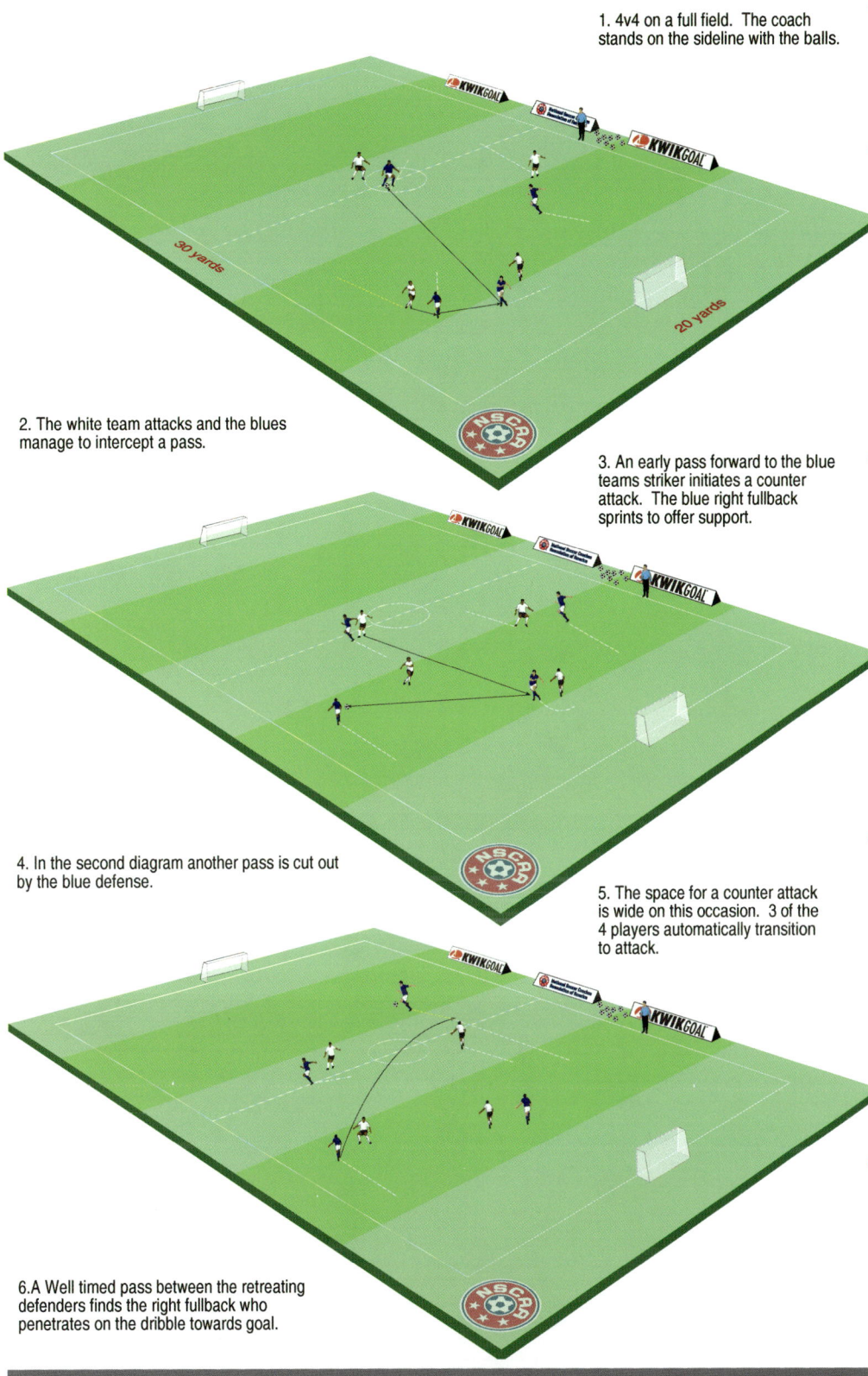

1. 4v4 on a full field. The coach stands on the sideline with the balls.

2. The white team attacks and the blues manage to intercept a pass.

3. An early pass forward to the blue teams striker initiates a counter attack. The blue right fullback sprints to offer support.

4. In the second diagram another pass is cut out by the blue defense.

5. The space for a counter attack is wide on this occasion. 3 of the 4 players automatically transition to attack.

6. A Well timed pass between the retreating defenders finds the right fullback who penetrates on the dribble towards goal.

Why use it?

A team without the ball will not be able to win so this game teaches teams how to move together to press the opposition all over the pitch and force a mistake.

Set up

This activity is played on a 4v4 field measuring 30x20 yards and two appropriate size goals are at each end. 2 teams of 4 players start in the coaches preferred formations. In this example the white team is set up in a diamond 0-1-2-1 and the blue team in 0-3-1. Balls can be placed next to the goals and/or the halfway line so the coach can initiate a restart from the goal line.

How to play

Both teams of 4 players attempt to score in the opponents goal. The 4v4 environment is excellent to teach young players to press and cover. Without a goalkeeper as the last line of defense, the players must make decisions whether to press high and attempt to win possession or drop back and protect the goal. All 4 players must work hard to deny space, cover and support their teammates. When a team successfully wins possession, they should spread out to make defending more difficult.

Coaching notes

Coaching Objectives: Recovery runs can now be addressed when the ball gets behind the defenders.
Coaching Tips: Coaches should focus on defenders reading cues before the ball is served; attempting to arrive as or before the receiver's first touch. Defenders should be taught to adopt an angle of approach that denies options and protects vulnerable areas (opponents, goal, passing lanes, etc.)

How to modify

Less Challenging: Require an attacking player or two to remain in their half of the field when transitioning to the attack. This condition will give the defenders more time to organize and less space to cover. A similar result can be achieved by insisting the defending team retreats to halfway or the attacking team must pass back to the central defender before advancing forward.
More Challenging: Give the defensive players 5 seconds to apply pressure or the opposition wins a point.

Stage/s of development covered by activity

Stages 2, 3 and 4 - 6-14 year old players.

Development themes and competencies

Top 3 themes: Defending positioning - pressure and cover, Defending as an individual, in pairs and small groups.
Top 3 competencies: Defensive stance, applying defensive pressure and communication.

BRING NSCAA COACHING EDUCATION TO YOUR COMMUNITY!

For more information visit **NSCAA.com/request-a-course** or call **816-471-1941.**

National Soccer Coaches Association of America

7v7 FORMATIONS - 1-2-1-3

Attacking Shape

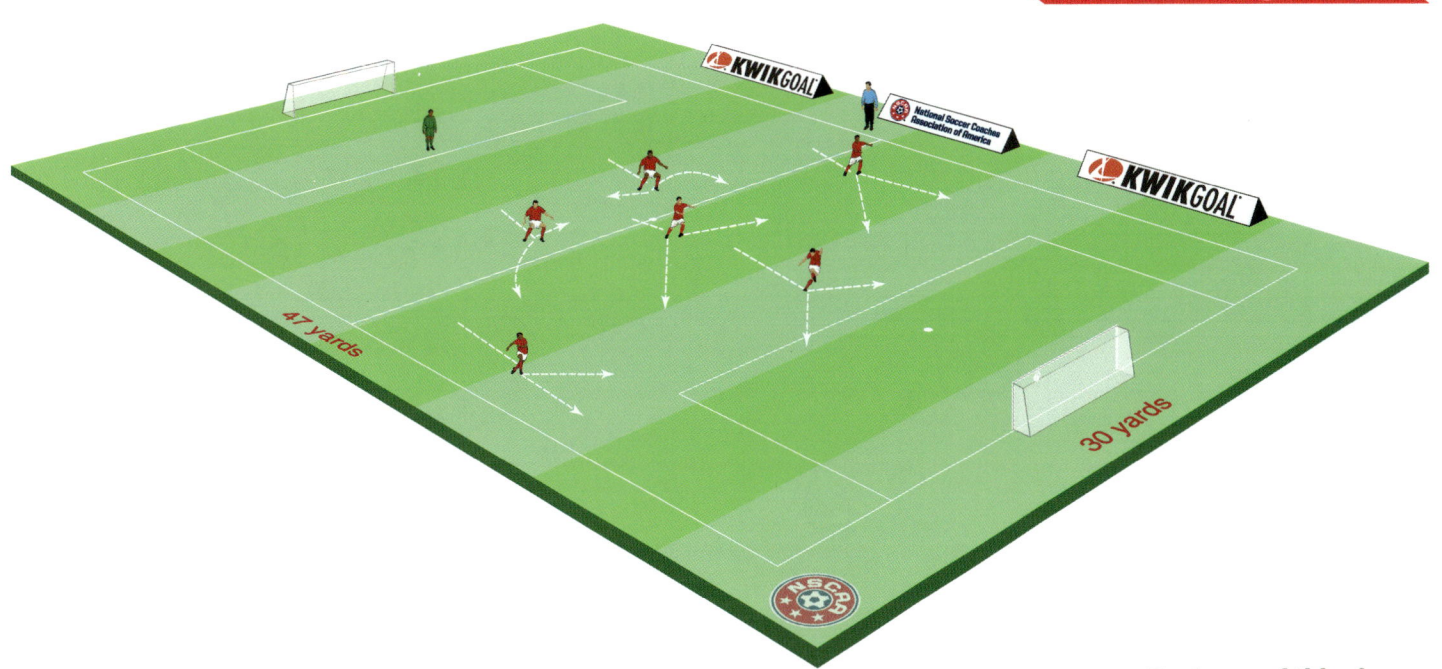

Features of this shape:

A natural progression from the 0-1-3 4v4 formation - adding 2 central defenders and a goalkeeper.
4 players always committed to the attack.
2 defenders provide cover for the midfield and attacking players allowing 4 players to fully commit to attack.
Wide attackers provide necessary width and the central striker should play high and penetrate behind the defense.

Defending Shape

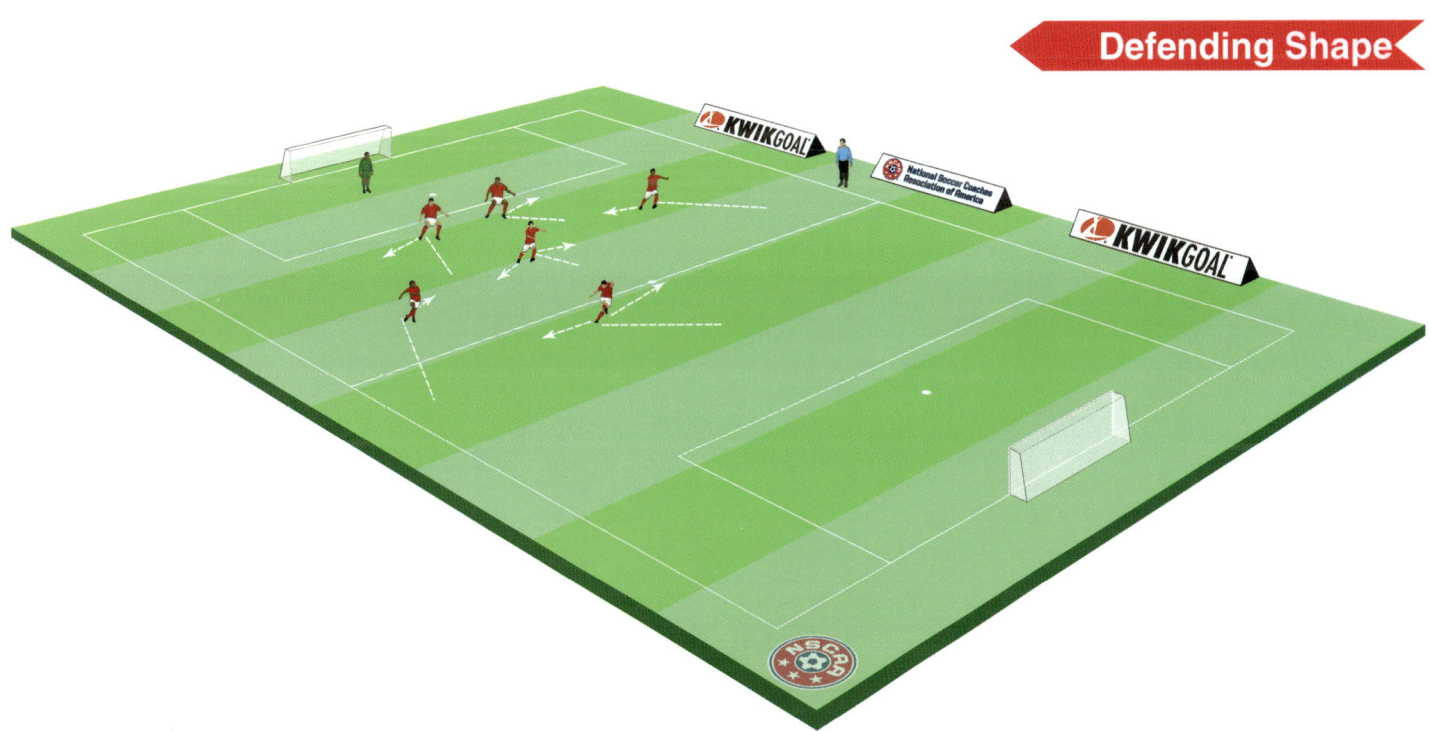

Features of this shape:

Two central defender are committed full-time to defending and drop to low pressure when possession is turned over - to reduce the space between the back line and the goalkeeper and allow attackers to recover.
Central midfield, left and right forwards must drop back towards the goal and provide cover and support
Striker moves laterally prevent the attacking team playing back to the defensive players.

7v7 FORMATIONS - 1-3-1-2

Attacking Shape

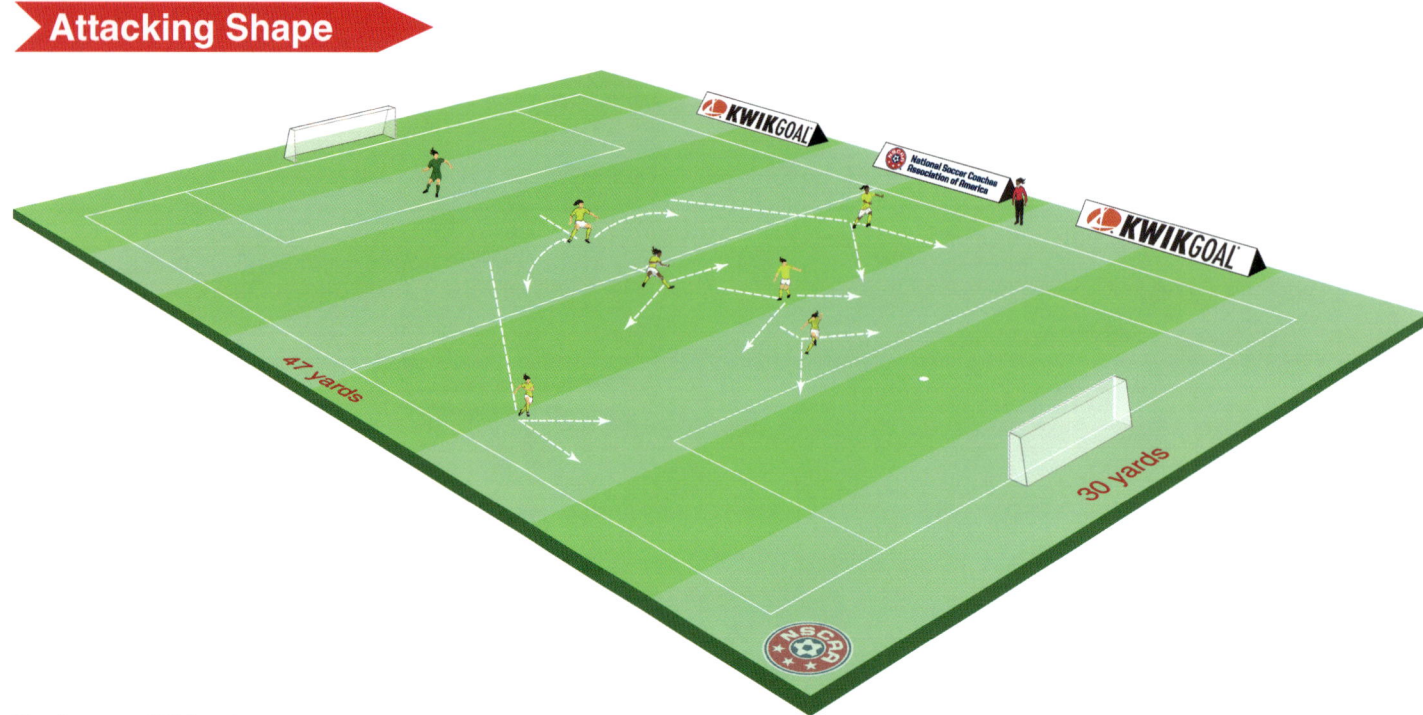

Features of this shape:
A slightly more aggressive attacking shape with 5 of the 6 outfield players committed to the attack.
The fullbacks move forward and provide the team with width - as the play develops down one flank the other fullback should tuck infield in case of a turnover and quick transition.
With 4 central players (defender, 1 midfield and 2 strikers) it is important to 'stretch' the opponent high.

Defending Shape

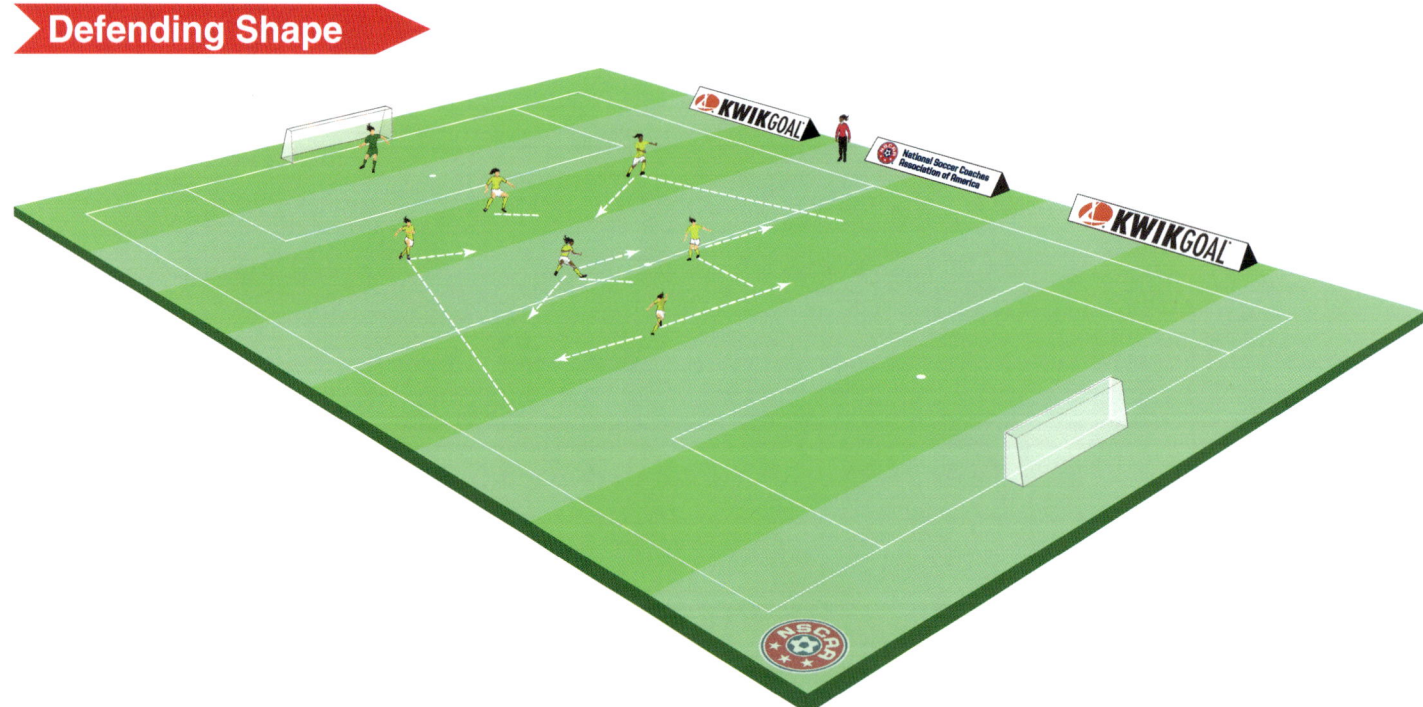

Features of this shape:
The left and right fullbacks must recover quickly or the lone central defender will be quickly exposed.
The central midfield player will likely be more defensive minded and must provide immediate support to the central defender.
The strikers must share responsibility to work back immediately possession is lost. Defend with at least 6.

7v7 FORMATIONS - 1-3-2-1

Attacking Shape

Features of this shape:
A slightly more cautious attacking formation with 2 central midfield players supporting the striker from deeper positions.
The fullbacks can be given greater freedom to attack than in 1-3-1-2, knowing there is an extra midfield player.
The striker must attempt to cut towards the ball from high positions, 'hold' possession and combine with midfield.

Defending Shape

Features of this shape:
The left and right fullbacks must recover quickly or the lone central defender will be quickly exposed.
The defensive central midfield player maybe the first player to support the central defender and can drop into the back line if needed.
Attacking midfield player's role should be to disrupt the opponent's possession and 'double team' the ball carrier.

4v2 TO 4v4 ATTACKING WIDTH - FUNCTIONAL

Why use it?
Creating space is attack can be achieved with a combination of player movement, dribbling penetration and intelligent passing. Attackers are encouraged in this activity to utilize the available width and create opportunities to play 'around' the defenders.

Set up
The set up is 35x30 yards with two cone gates located at both end of the field approximately 5 yards from the center. A good supply of balls are placed just outside the 4 corners of the area and the coach observes from the sideline. Commence the activity with a 4v2 and progress to 4v4.

How to play
The team with 4 players starts with one of the players collecting a ball from a pile in a corner. The player on the ball dribbles into the area and the game is live. The objective for both teams is to score through the opponent's cone goals. As a consequence of the goal location, it is likely the 2 defenders will drop deep and become compact around the goals allowing the attackers time and space. Providing the defenders with an attacking objective is important to 'draw' the defenders out to the ball carrier. Using the full width of the field the attacking team should attempt to move the ball quickly and attack around the outside of the defenders. If the defenders win possession they must counter attack and attempt to score at the other end. The activity is played in 8x2 minute intervals, with a 30-60 second break in between each interval. During intervals 1-4 the goals have different point values - 1 point for passing through the left goal and 2 points for dribbling through the right goal. For intervals 4-8, the coach imposes a rule that a player receiving a ball with back-to-goal cannot turn.

Coaching notes
Coaching Objectives: Creating space as an individual and team is the main theme of the activity. Wide players should move to the perimeter and open their bodies on receipt of the ball. The central attacker should move 'high' up the field to create depth and height.
Coaching Tip: Positioning balls in the corners allows the attacking team to restart the game and establish an attacking tempo. On occasions a quick restart may catch the defenders in transition.

How to modify
Less Challenging: Commence the activity with a numerical advantage for the attacking team. Create more space by moving the boundaries of the area wider.
More Challenging: Add minimum touch restrictions for the attackers to slow down the attack and allow the defenders to recover. Also impose the 'no turn' rule to force the striker to play 'high'.

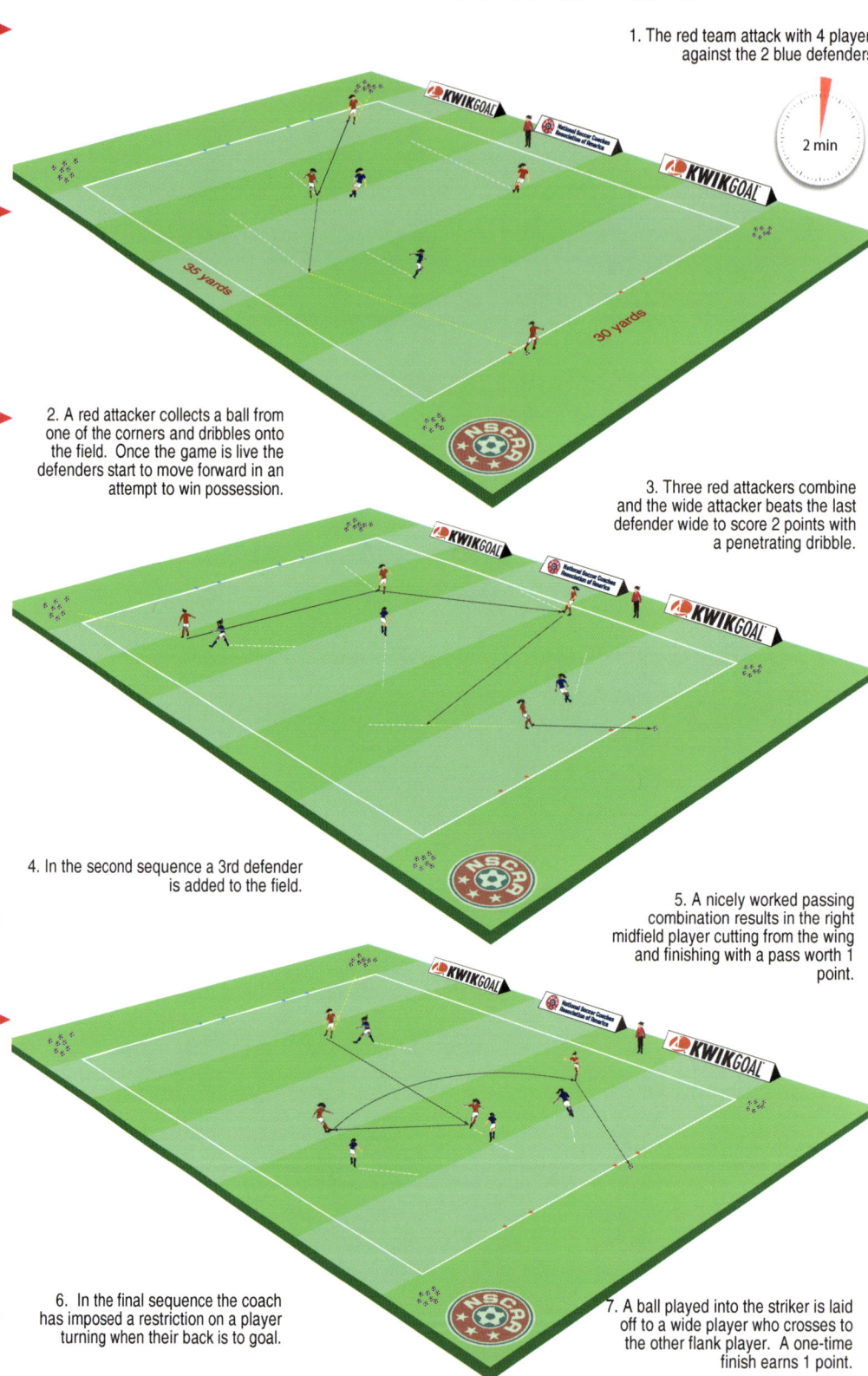

1. The red team attack with 4 players against the 2 blue defenders.
2. A red attacker collects a ball from one of the corners and dribbles onto the field. Once the game is live the defenders start to move forward in an attempt to win possession.
3. Three red attackers combine and the wide attacker beats the last defender wide to score 2 points with a penetrating dribble.
4. In the second sequence a 3rd defender is added to the field.
5. A nicely worked passing combination results in the right midfield player cutting from the wing and finishing with a pass worth 1 point.
6. In the final sequence the coach has imposed a restriction on a player turning when their back is to goal.
7. A ball played into the striker is laid off to a wide player who crosses to the other flank player. A one-time finish earns 1 point.

Stage/s of development covered by activity
Stages 3, 4 and 5 - 9-18 year old players.

Development themes and competencies
Top 3 Themes: Passing technique, creating space as an individual/team and defending (pressure and cover).
Top 3 Competencies: 1v1 attacking, passing over short/medium distances and movement off the ball.

5v3 TO 5v6 ATTACKING WIDTH - PHASE OF PLAY

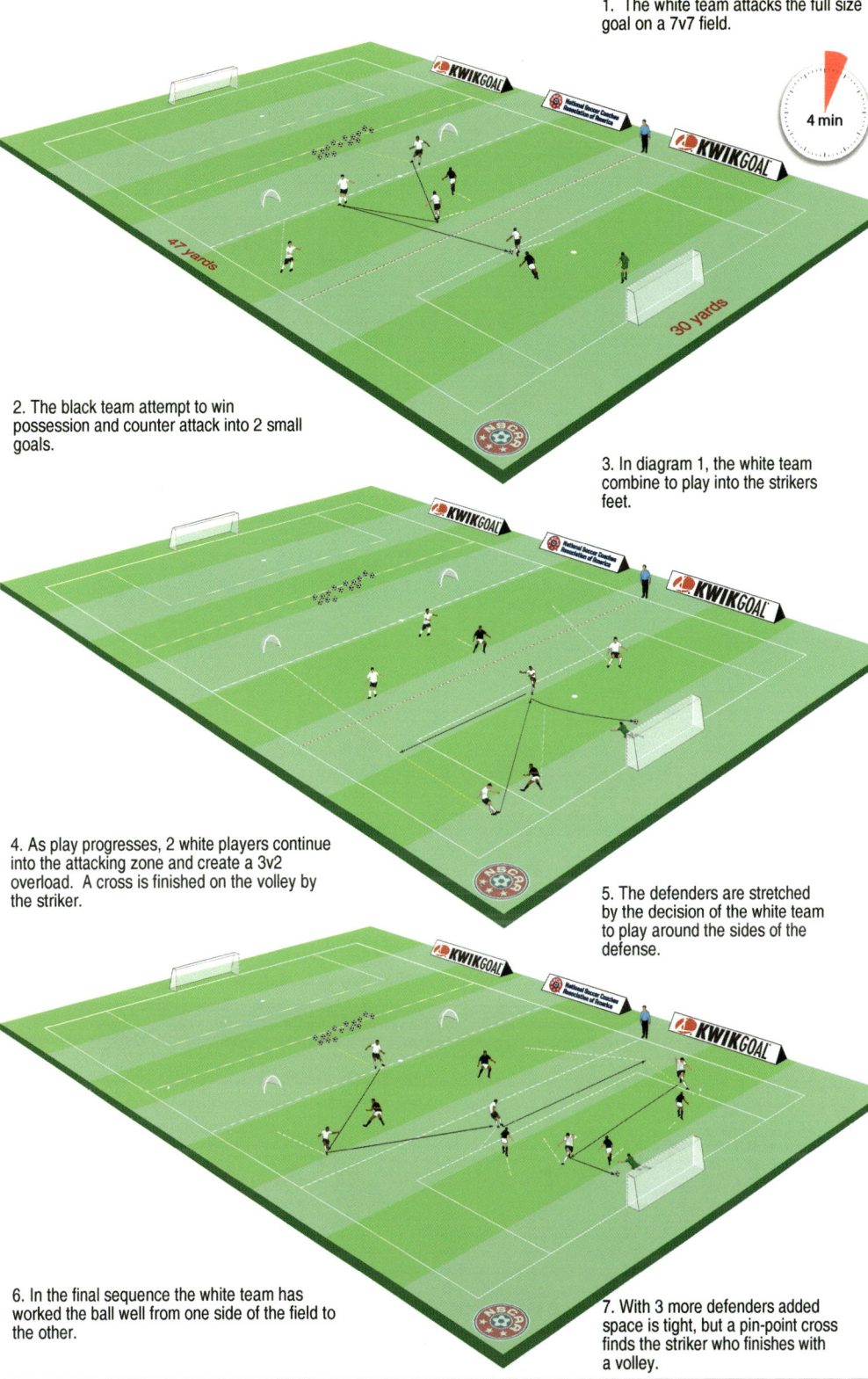

1. The white team attacks the full size goal on a 7v7 field.

2. The black team attempt to win possession and counter attack into 2 small goals.

3. In diagram 1, the white team combine to play into the strikers feet.

4. As play progresses, 2 white players continue into the attacking zone and create a 3v2 overload. A cross is finished on the volley by the striker.

5. The defenders are stretched by the decision of the white team to play around the sides of the defense.

6. In the final sequence the white team has worked the ball well from one side of the field to the other.

7. With 3 more defenders added space is tight, but a pin-point cross finds the striker who finishes with a volley.

Why use it?

This is a phase of play activity involving midfield and forward players on the attacking team. The attacking focus is to build up play through 2 lines of the team by playing around the defenders.

Set up

The set up is 47x30 yards full 7v7 field. Played in approximately two thirds of the field, a large supply of balls are placed at one end of the field close to the restraining line. 2 small goals are set up as counter attacking options for the defending team midway between the restraining line and halfway and an appropriate size goal is at the other end. The restraining line, 16 yards from the end line separates 2 zones of the field. In the zone closest to the small goals commence with 4v1 in favor of the attackers and in the attacking zone play 1 attacker against a defender and a goalkeeper.

How to play

One of the attackers collects a ball from the pile and dribbles or passes to a teammate. Playing 4v1 should result in high passing success for the attackers. The attacking objective is to pass the ball to the striker and then for the midfield players to join into the attack. To begin the coach imposes a restriction on the defender in the attacking third - if a pass is made to the striker, the defender must permit the striker to receive the ball before playing high pressure. 2 midfield players are permitted to support the attacker once a pass is made to create a 3v2 overload. Play 4 intervals each 4 minutes in length. Intervals 1 & 2 - allow 2 attackers to join the striker, 3 - allow 2 defenders to recover, 4 - remove zonal restrictions and allow defenders to deny the pass.

Coaching notes

Coaching Objectives: Stress the importance of stretching the defenders wide and high to create more space.
Coaching Tip: Imposing a condition preventing a defender denying a pass to the striker ensures the defender in the other half will 'press' the ball in an attempt to win possession before the pass is made.

How to modify

Less Challenging: Start with patterns of play and remove the defender.
More Challenging: Add more defenders and remove all restrictions on the defenders.

Stage/s of development covered by activity

Stages 3, 4 and 5 - 9-18 year old players.

Development themes and competencies

Top 3 Themes: Passing technique, creating space as an individual/team and defending (pressure and cover).
Top 3 Competencies: 1v1 attacking, passing over short/medium distances and movement off the ball.

7v7 ATTACKING WIDTH GAME

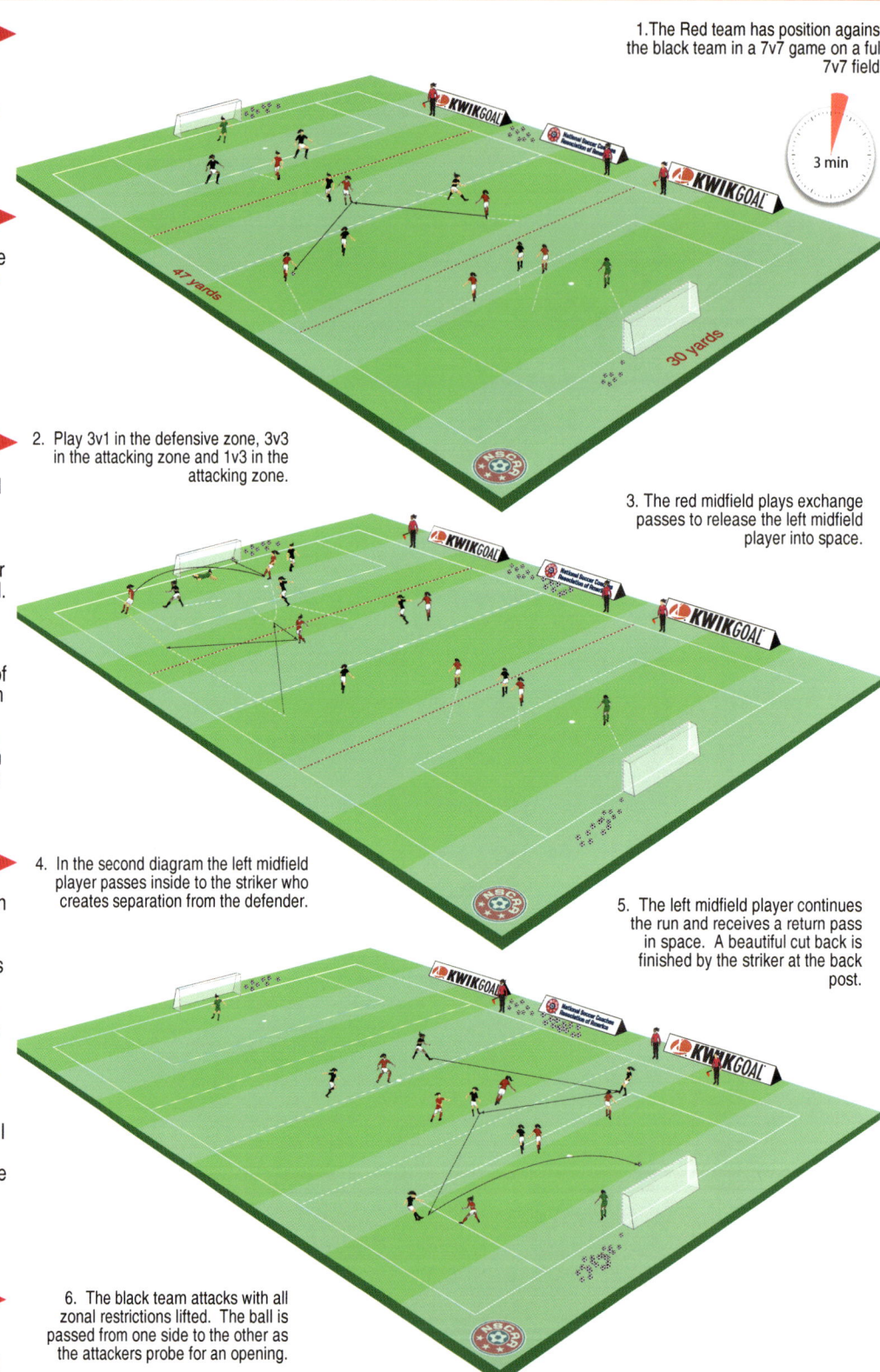

Why use it?
The third activity in the 'creating space series' is played on a full 7v7 field with both teams at full strength. Players must attempt to build up play from the goalkeeper to the striker whilst maintaining width, depth and height of the attack.

Set up
The set up is full 7v7 field with an appropriate size goal at both ends. The restraining lines at both ends are used to split the field into 3 zones. Play 3v1 in favor of the defenders in the defending end zones and 3v3 in the middle zone. The coach observes from the sideline and is supported by 2 assistants monitoring offside.

How to play
To begin the activity all players are restricted to the zones they start in. However, if an attacking player is successful in passing to the striker in the end zone that player is permitted to join the attack. The objective for both teams is to score in the opponent's goal. With a numerical advantage in the defense end, the attacking team should attempt to build-up play around the 'outside' of the defensive team. To increase the likelihood of the attack reaching the striker, the coach can restrict the defenders from denying a pass from the middle zone. Play 6 intervals each lasting 3 minutes. Intervals 1 and 2 maintain zone restrictions. Intervals allow 1-2 players to move freely between zones and Intervals 5 and 6 remove all restrictions.

Coaching notes
Coaching Objectives: A players body position as the ball is travelling will often determine the choices available once the ball arrives. An 'open' body position maximizes a player's options and increases a player's ability to scan the field. A pass made into the path of a player can permit the attacker to penetrate into space with one touch. Moving to the sideline further reduces the amount of 'dead space' and typically creates more time for decision making.
Coaching Tip: If the players are unsuccessful in playing the ball 'around' the other team, consider adding some cones to create a wide channel on one or both sides. Allow only attacking players to enter the wide areas to provide some time and space for the attack to develop.

How to modify
Less Challenging: Commence the activity with a numerical advantage for the attacking team. Allow the attacking team only to move freely between zones. Add wide channels to encourage players to get wide.
More Challenging: Play with both teams at full strength with no restrictions.

1. The Red team has position against the black team in a 7v7 game on a full 7v7 field.

2. Play 3v1 in the defensive zone, 3v3 in the attacking zone and 1v3 in the attacking zone.

3. The red midfield plays exchange passes to release the left midfield player into space.

4. In the second diagram the left midfield player passes inside to the striker who creates separation from the defender.

5. The left midfield player continues the run and receives a return pass in space. A beautiful cut back is finished by the striker at the back post.

6. The black team attacks with all zonal restrictions lifted. The ball is passed from one side to the other as the attackers probe for an opening.

Stage/s of development covered by activity
Stages 3, 4 and 5 - 9-18 year old players.

Development themes and competencies

Top 3 Themes: Passing technique, creating space as an individual/team and defending (pressure and cover).
Top 3 Competencies: 1v1 attacking, passing over short/medium distances and movement off the ball.

PENETRATION 6v3 TO 6v6 FUNCTIONAL

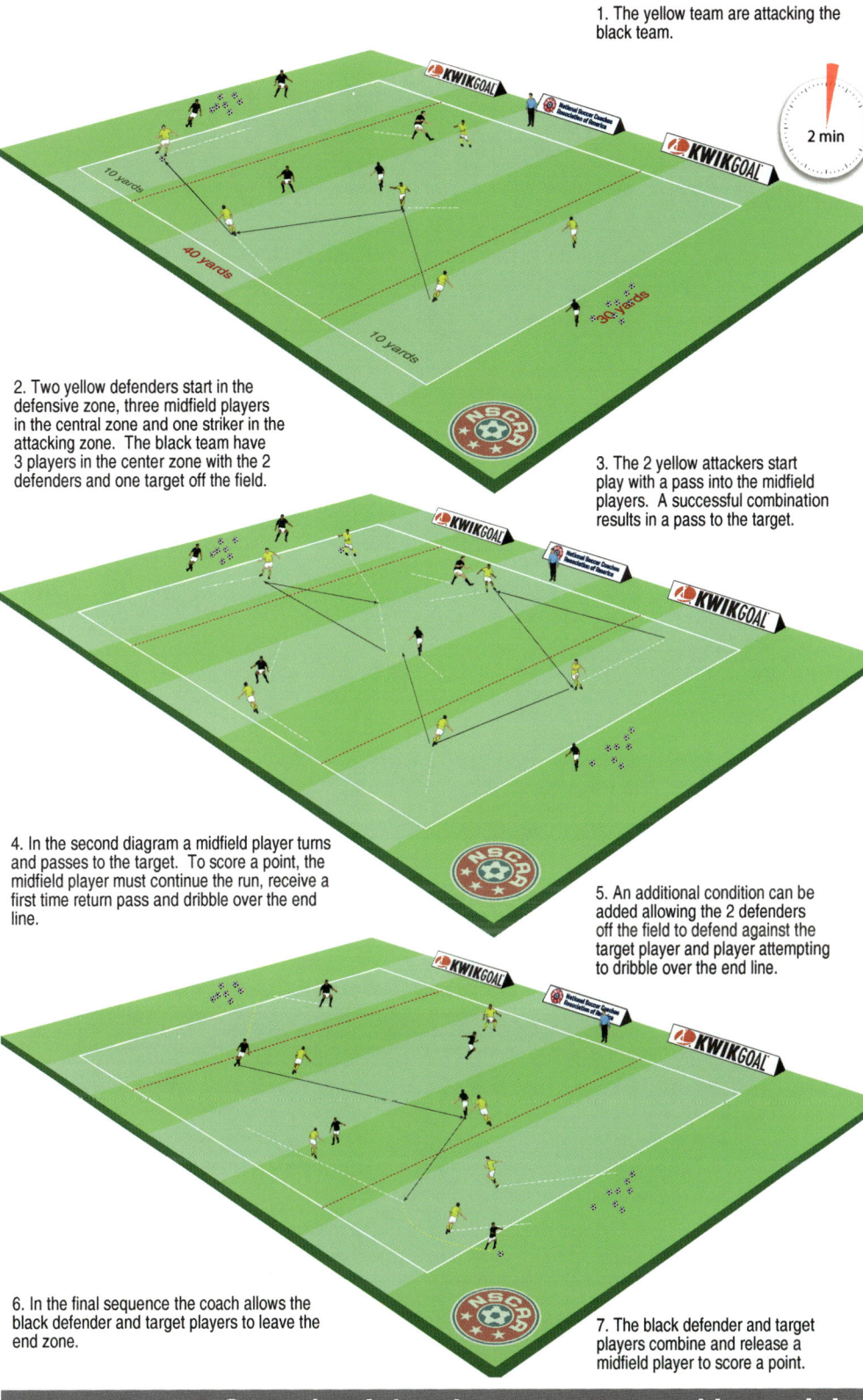

1. The yellow team are attacking the black team.

2. Two yellow defenders start in the defensive zone, three midfield players in the central zone and one striker in the attacking zone. The black team have 3 players in the center zone with the 2 defenders and one target off the field.

3. The 2 yellow attackers start play with a pass into the midfield players. A successful combination results in a pass to the target.

4. In the second diagram a midfield player turns and passes to the target. To score a point, the midfield player must continue the run, receive a first time return pass and dribble over the end line.

5. An additional condition can be added allowing the 2 defenders off the field to defend against the target player and player attempting to dribble over the end line.

6. In the final sequence the coach allows the black defender and target players to leave the end zone.

7. The black defender and target players combine and release a midfield player to score a point.

Stage/s of development covered by activity
Stages 3, 4 and 5 - 9-18 year old players.

Development themes and competencies
Top 3 Themes: Passing technique, possession and creating space as an individual/team.
Top 3 Competencies: Passing over short/medium distances, communication and movement off the ball.

Why use it?
The players will enjoy this fast paced, back and forth activity focusing on penetration and possession. The coach can introduce a number of variations to increase the complexity and challenge as players become more competent.

Set up
The set up is 40x30 yards rectangle with a 10x30 yards end zone at each end of the area. A supply of balls is located outside the 2 end zones and the coach stands on the sideline to observe. 2 teams of 6 players attempt to play to a target player to score a point. The team in possession of the ball starts with 2 players in the defending end zone, 3 players in the middle zone and 1 target in the attacking end zone. The team without possession has a similar set up, although the players in the end zones must step out of the end zone when the opponent has the ball.

How to play
The coach determines which team has possession and one of the defending players collects a ball from the pile outside the end zone. At the start, all the players must remain in the zone in which they started. The team with possession has a 6v3 numerical advantage. The attacking objective is to play around, through or over the central defenders and play the ball to the target player. If the defending team is able to intercept the ball, the players in the end zone quickly transition, with one team entering and one team leaving the area. Each time a pass is made to the target player the team earns a point. Play is restarted with the 2 defenders after a successful pass is made to the target - teams only attack in one direction. As the game progresses, the coach can add additional conditions to challenge the attacking players.

Coaching notes
Coaching Objectives: Attacking players must work to create space with quick ball movement and runs off the ball. Faced with a compact defense the attackers should seek to play 'around' the outside. The target player should be encouraged to move along the end zone.
Coaching Tip: Zones are useful for a coach to provide time and space for decision making.

How to modify
Less Challenging: Start with pattern play.
More Challenging: Make the area narrower and allow players to leave the zones.

PENETRATION 5v4 THROUGH AROUND OR OVER PHASE

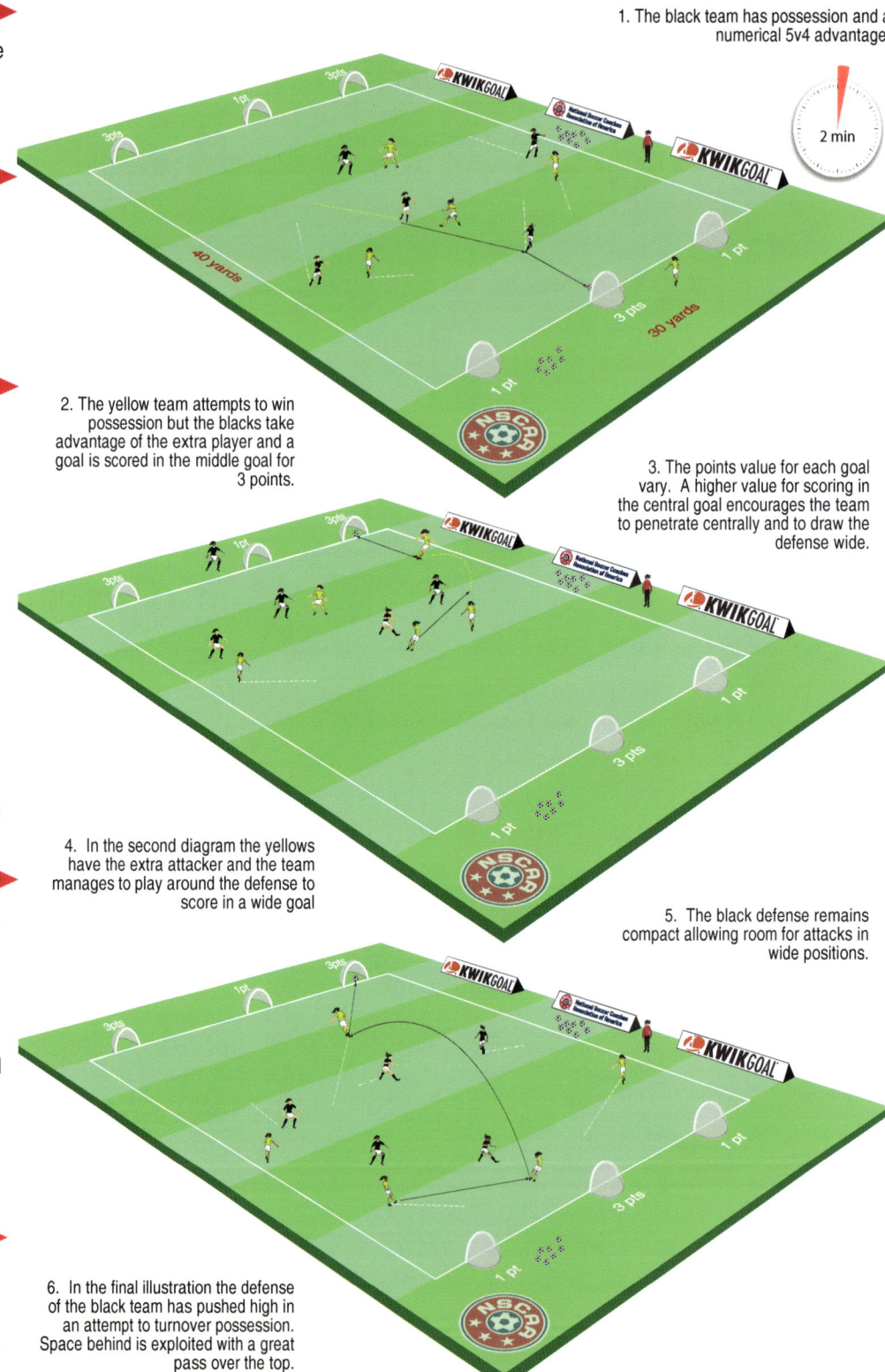

Why use it?
This is a phase of play activity involving three lines of the team, namely, defense, midfield and forwards. The attacking team must use a numerical advantage to score in three goals with varying points value.

Set up
The set up is a 40x30 yards area with 3 mini goals placed along the end line at each end. One goal is in the center of the line and the other 2 wide goals are 4 yards from the sideline. The team with possession has a numerical 5v4 advantage. The coach observes from the sideline.

How to play
The primary objective is for the team in possession of the ball to determine the best strategy to score goals. To add an extra degree of challenge the goals are worth different points values. The attacking team should seek to maximize the size of the area sending players wide, high and deep. The options are to play around the 'edges' and penetrate wide, pass down the seams between defenders and/or play over the defense into space vacated behind. If the defenders win possession a player from the attacking team steps off the field and a player for the defending team steps on to create a 5v4. Play 6 intervals each lasting 2 minutes. Intervals 1-2 maintain 5v4 numerical advantage. Intervals 3-4 add an extra defender to create 5v5 and intervals 5-6 make the central goal worth 3 points and the outside goals worth 1 point.

Coaching notes
Coaching Objectives: Assist players to read the visual cues that determine which is the best strategy to exploit weaknesses in the defense. With only 4 players, the defense is outnumbered so the attackers must communicate effectively to coordinate ball and player movements.
Coaching Tip: Providing a points system will help the coach to direct a particular game strategy. For example, telling the players that a goal scored in a wide goal is worth 3 points and a goal scored in the center is worth 1 point should lead to the attackers spreading play wide.

How to modify
Less Challenging: Reduce the number of defenders further. The coach can also add a restraining line to prevent the defenders pushing too high, wide or dropping too deep.
More Challenging: Change the values of the goals and only inform the attacking team.

1. The black team has possession and a numerical 5v4 advantage.

2. The yellow team attempts to win possession but the blacks take advantage of the extra player and a goal is scored in the middle goal for 3 points.

3. The points value for each goal vary. A higher value for scoring in the central goal encourages the team to penetrate centrally and to draw the defense wide.

4. In the second diagram the yellows have the extra attacker and the team manages to play around the defense to score in a wide goal

5. The black defense remains compact allowing room for attacks in wide positions.

6. In the final illustration the defense of the black team has pushed high in an attempt to turnover possession. Space behind is exploited with a great pass over the top.

Stage/s of development covered by activity
Stages 3, 4 and 5 - 9-18 year old players.

Development themes and competencies
Top 3 Themes: Passing technique, possession and creating space as an individual/team.
Top 3 Competencies: Passing over short/medium distances, communication and movement off the ball.

PENETRATION 7v7 THROUGH AROUND OR OVER GAME

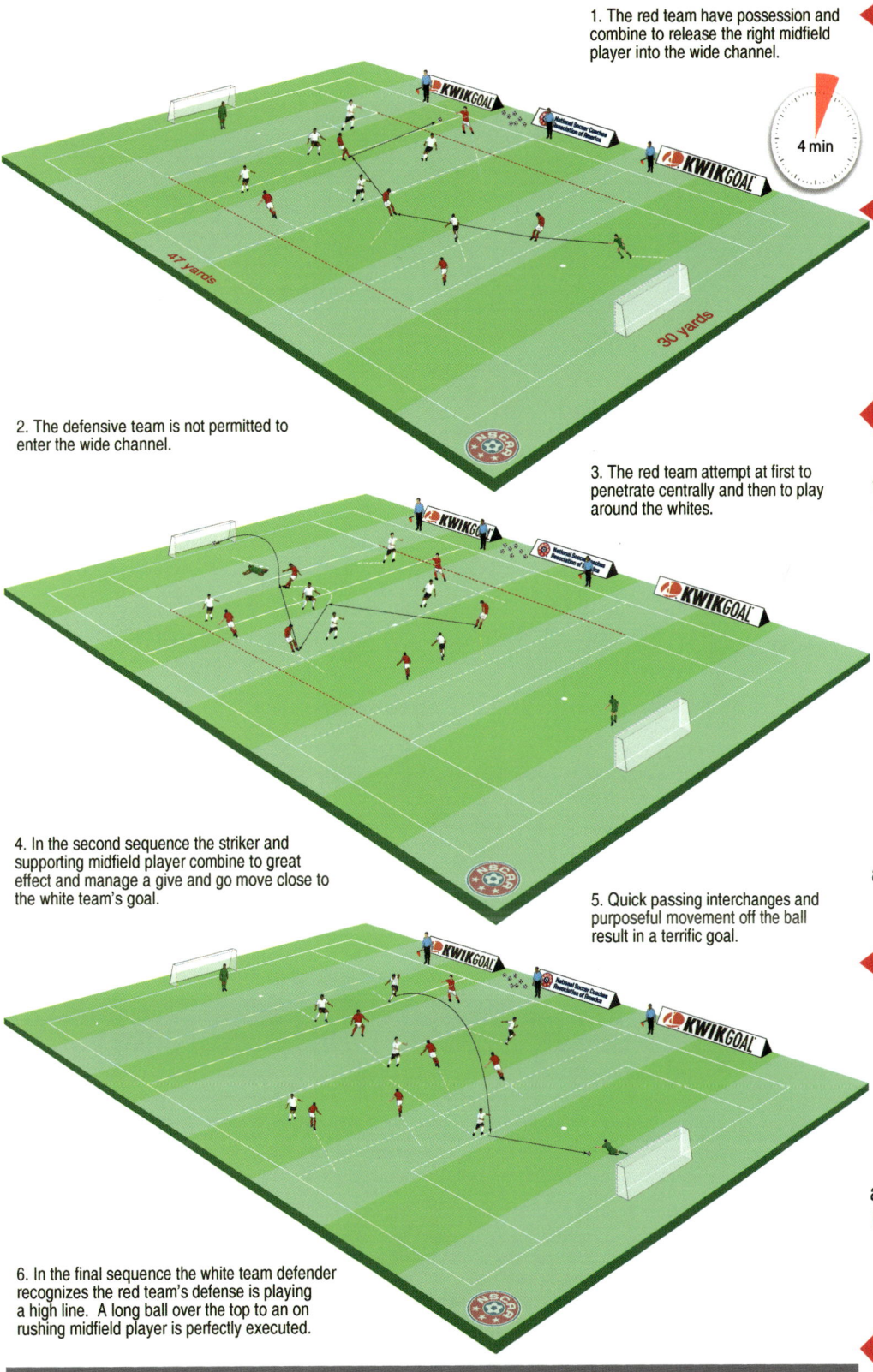

1. The red team have possession and combine to release the right midfield player into the wide channel.

2. The defensive team is not permitted to enter the wide channel.

3. The red team attempt at first to penetrate centrally and then to play around the whites.

4. In the second sequence the striker and supporting midfield player combine to great effect and manage a give and go move close to the white team's goal.

5. Quick passing interchanges and purposeful movement off the ball result in a terrific goal.

6. In the final sequence the white team defender recognizes the red team's defense is playing a high line. A long ball over the top to an on rushing midfield player is perfectly executed.

Why use it?

This activity emphasizes wide play and the opportunity to deliver crosses into the opponent's penalty area. The coach can simply modify the challenge by increasing or deceasing the magnitude of defensive pressure.

Set up

The set up is full 7v7 field with an appropriate size goal at both ends. A wide channel is marked on both sides of the field with cones. The coach observes from the sideline and is supported by 2 assistants monitoring offside.

How to play

Commence the game playing with the typical rules for this 7v7 game format. The objective is for each team to penetrate the opponent's defense by playing 'around', 'through' or 'over'. The attacking channels emphasize the importance of width and provide the attacking team with a goal of stretching the defense wide. Allow only attacking players to enter the channels to begin as the ball is played. It is likely the defending team will be stretched horizontally to press the attacking team's width and this will create space to play into the central midfield players and striker. To highlight the attacking role of the center midfield player, the coach can award 2 points for a goal scored when the central player is involved in the attack. This change of focus will also raise the importance of playing 'through' and between the seams of the defense.

Coaching notes

Coaching Objectives: Attacking players must work to create space with quick ball movement and runs off the ball. Faced with a compact defense the attackers should seek to play 'around' the outside.
Coaching Tip: On occasion, a wide channel may unintentionally result in unrealistic play, such as, slowing down for a measured cross without a threat of losing possession to a defender. To this end, the coach can add additional conditions such as an allowable time limit for an attacker with the ball or a touch limit inside the channel.

How to modify

Less Challenging: Reduce the number of defenders and maintain the channel restrictions in favor of the attackers.
More Challenging: Remove the wide channels and require a player to be included in all attacking sequences.

Stage/s of development covered by activity

Stages 3, 4 and 5 - 9-18 year old players.

Development themes and competencies

Top 3 Themes: Passing technique, possession and creating space as an individual/team.
Top 3 Competencies: Passing over short/medium distances, communication and movement off the ball.

1v1 TO 2v2 PRESSURE AND COVER DEFENDING - FUNCTIONAL

Why use it?
This is an introductory activity to teach young players the role of the first or pressure defender. As the player becomes more proficient at defending, the coach can add an additional attacker and defender. This development enables the coach to also teach the role of the second or cover defender.

Set up
The set up is a 38x30 yards area separated into two adjacent fields 38x15 yards. Each field has 3 zones with the end zones 12 yards in length and the middle zone 14 yards in length. A supply of balls is placed outside the end line of each area to allow the players to restart the game continuously. On each field there are 4 players, 2 in the middle zone and 1 at each end acting as a server. The server must remain outside the area to begin the activity. The coach is on the sideline.

How to play
The focus of this activity is individual and pairs defending, although the activity will work equally well with an attacking theme. The objective for the attacking players is to score by dribbling over the end zone lines. The game commences with a pass from one of the servers to the feet of the attacker. The attacker must attempt to turn and dribble to the opposite end. The first defender must try and prevent the attacker turning and dribbling. In the event of an interception the defender should pass to the server to score a point. If the attacker is successful in beating the first defender in the middle zone, the server at the back of the end zone should come forward and try to deny the attacker dribbling across the back line. The first defender in the middle zone is not allowed to enter the end zone. If the defending player in the end zone successfully wins the ball the team of 2 should counter attack and attempt to score at the other end. Play 10 intervals each lasting 30 seconds. Intervals 1-4 play 1v1 and switch roles each interval. Intervals 5-7 allow the attacking team to have two players in middle zone to create a 2v1. If the defender in the middle wins the ball, the teammate joins in and the attacking team sends a player back to the end zone to create a 2v1 the other way. Intervals 8-10 play 2v2.

Coaching notes
Coaching Objectives: Teach the first defender to close space, lower body, side ways positioning and patience.
Coaching Tip: Time working on defending is well spent. Young players will often 'fly' into a challenge to win the ball and will be off balance.

How to modify
Less Challenging: Keep the activity 1v1 until the player has achieved some success.
More Challenging: Move to 2v1 in favor of the attackers and work on the defenders decision making.

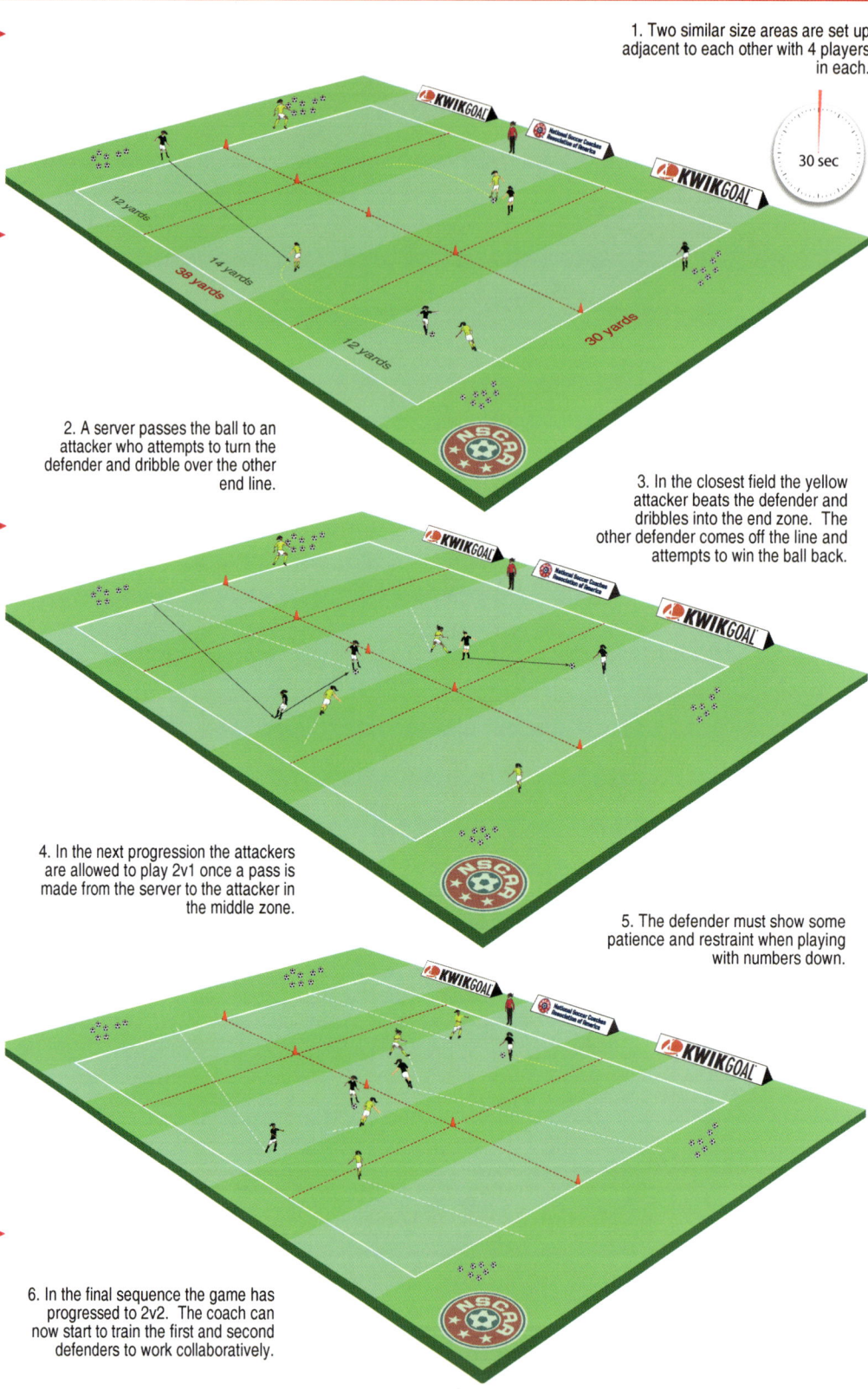

1. Two similar size areas are set up adjacent to each other with 4 players in each.

2. A server passes the ball to an attacker who attempts to turn the defender and dribble over the other end line.

3. In the closest field the yellow attacker beats the defender and dribbles into the end zone. The other defender comes off the line and attempts to win the ball back.

4. In the next progression the attackers are allowed to play 2v1 once a pass is made from the server to the attacker in the middle zone.

5. The defender must show some patience and restraint when playing with numbers down.

6. In the final sequence the game has progressed to 2v2. The coach can now start to train the first and second defenders to work collaboratively.

Stage/s of development covered by activity
Stages 2, 3, 4 and 5 - 6-18 year old players.

Development themes and competencies
Top 3 Themes: Individual and pairs defending, 1v1 attacking and communication.
Top 3 Competencies: Defending pressure, defending cover and defending recovery.

4v4 PRESSURE, COVER, BALANCE DEFENDING - PHASE

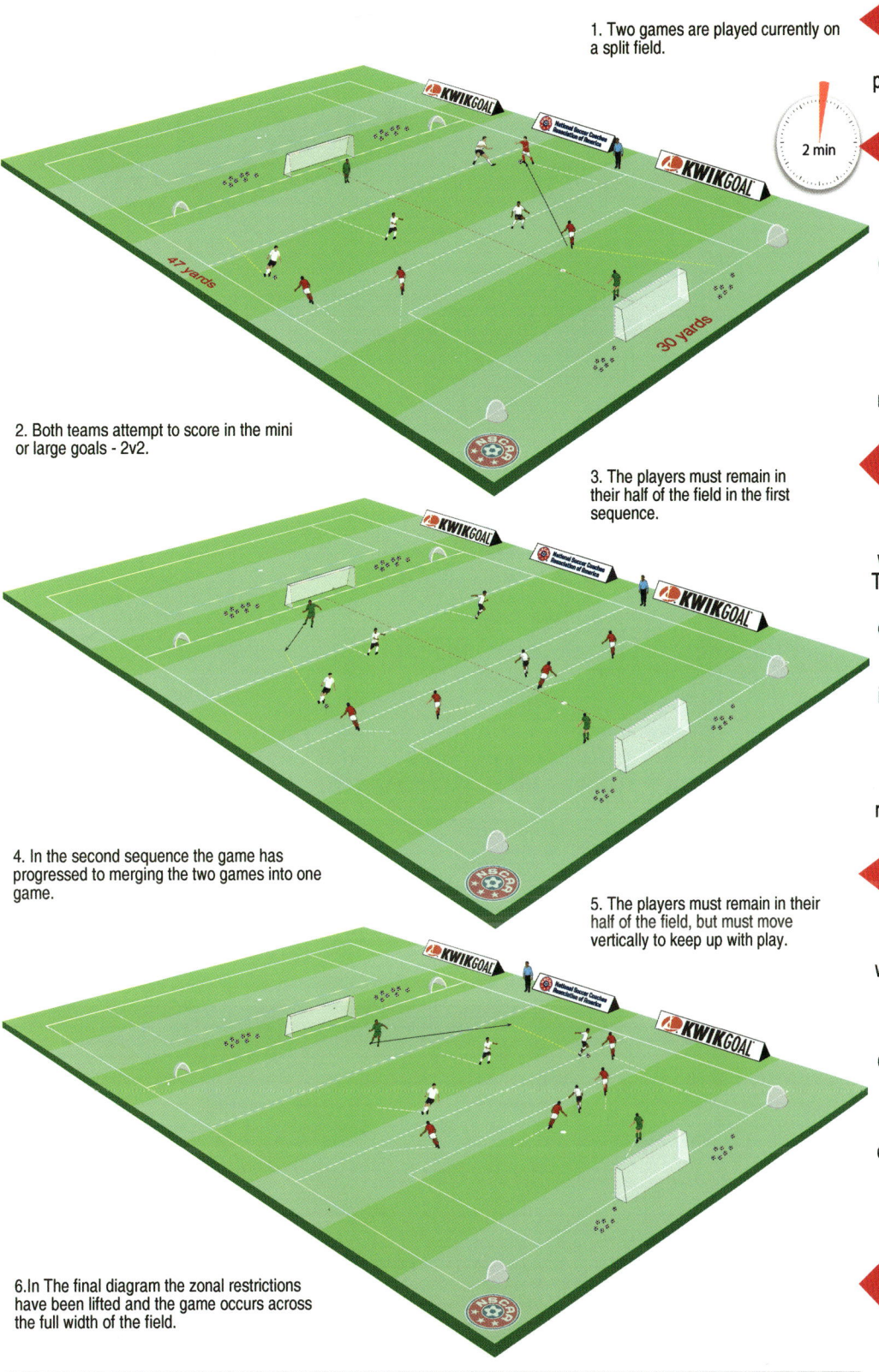

1. Two games are played currently on a split field.

2. Both teams attempt to score in the mini or large goals - 2v2.

3. The players must remain in their half of the field in the first sequence.

4. In the second sequence the game has progressed to merging the two games into one game.

5. The players must remain in their half of the field, but must move vertically to keep up with play.

6. In The final diagram the zonal restrictions have been lifted and the game occurs across the full width of the field.

Why use it?

This activity continues the theme of pressure and cover defending with specific focus on defending in wide areas.

Set up

The set up is a 30x30 yards area played on a 7v7 field - use the restraining line at one end as the end line. The field is also divided into two to create a 'left' and 'right' field. On each end line are 2 mini goals close to the sidelines and a full size goal with a goalkeeper. On each side of the field play 2v2. A supply of balls is placed near each goal to allow the keepers to restart the game continuously. The coach observes from the sideline.

How to play

The focus of this activity is individual and pairs defending, although the activity will work equally well with an attacking theme. The objective for the attacking players is to score in either mini goals or large goal on one side of the field. The objective for the defending team is to win possession and counter attack to the other goals. Play 6 intervals each lasting 2 minutes. Intervals 1-2 play a game of 2v2 in each half of the field. Intervals 3-4 play with one ball but players are restricted to the side of the field in which they started. Intervals 5-6 remove the zonal restrictions and play 4v4 in the full width of the field.

Coaching notes

Coaching Objectives: Coaches can teach the roles of the first and second defender with particular emphasis on preventing the opponent from penetrating the defense. As the games are merged the coach can also introduce the role of the 3rd and 4th defenders in providing cover and balance.
Coaching Tip: Encourage the young defenders to apply pressure high enough up the field to prevent the opponent from entering shooting range. When the player has an opportunity to force the attacker away from goal they should apply high pressure. This is often sufficient for a young attacker to give up possession.

How to modify

Less Challenging: Start with 1v1 and progress to 2v2 once the defenders are experiencing success.
More Challenging: Progress by removing the zonal restrictions earlier in the session and impose a time restriction on the attack. This condition will add urgency to the attack and will require on more intense effort from the defenders.

Stage/s of development covered by activity
Stages 3, 4 and 5 - 9-18 year old players.

Development themes and competencies
Top 3 Themes: Individual and pairs defending, transition and communication.
Top 3 Competencies: Defending pressure, defending cover and defending recovery.

7v7 PRESSURE, COVER, BALANCE DEFENDING - GAME

Why use it?

A 7v7 game designed to teach the players to play high and low press defense as an individual and team. Working with the players to recognize visual cues and communication between teammates are key considerations.

Set up

The set up is full 7v7 field with an appropriate size goal at both ends. The field is separated at halfway into two zones. Around each goal is a 5 yards 'keeper only' zone. Play 7v7. The coach observes from the sideline and is supported by 2 assistants monitoring offside.

How to play

Each team is allowed 2 central midfield players to move freely between the 2 zones and all others are restricted to the zone they started in. The attacking objective is to pass the ball to the other team's goalkeeper, either on the ground or in the air. Goalkeepers are restricted to the 'keeper zone'. The goalkeeper earns a point for each ball they catch or collect clean. The primary objective for the defense is to prevent the attacking team from passing to the goalkeeper. Play 6 intervals each lasting 3 minutes. To encourage the defense to press early and high up the field, award the attacking team 3 points if the ball is passed to the goal keeper from the defending half. Award 1 point if the ball is played from the attacking half (Intervals 1-2). To encourage defenders to deny space in the attacking half reverse the scoring - 1 point if the ball is passed to the goalkeeper from the defending half and 3 points if the ball is played from the attacking half (Intervals 3-4). Remove all the restrictions for intervals 5-6 to see if the players can read the cues.

Coaching notes

Coaching Objectives: The coach should encourage defenders to press the player in possession early and for the team to remain compact. Work with players to recognize the visual cues to determine if the player on the ball will play short or long.
Coaching Tip: The coach can introduce a points system (as described above) to provide extra emphasis on the type of strategy the coach wants to see employed. Introduce the idea of defending early or later.

How to modify

Less Challenging: Reduce the number of attacking players and reduce the size of the field.
More Challenging: Use the larger penalty box as the 'keeper zone' and play with full 7v7 teams.

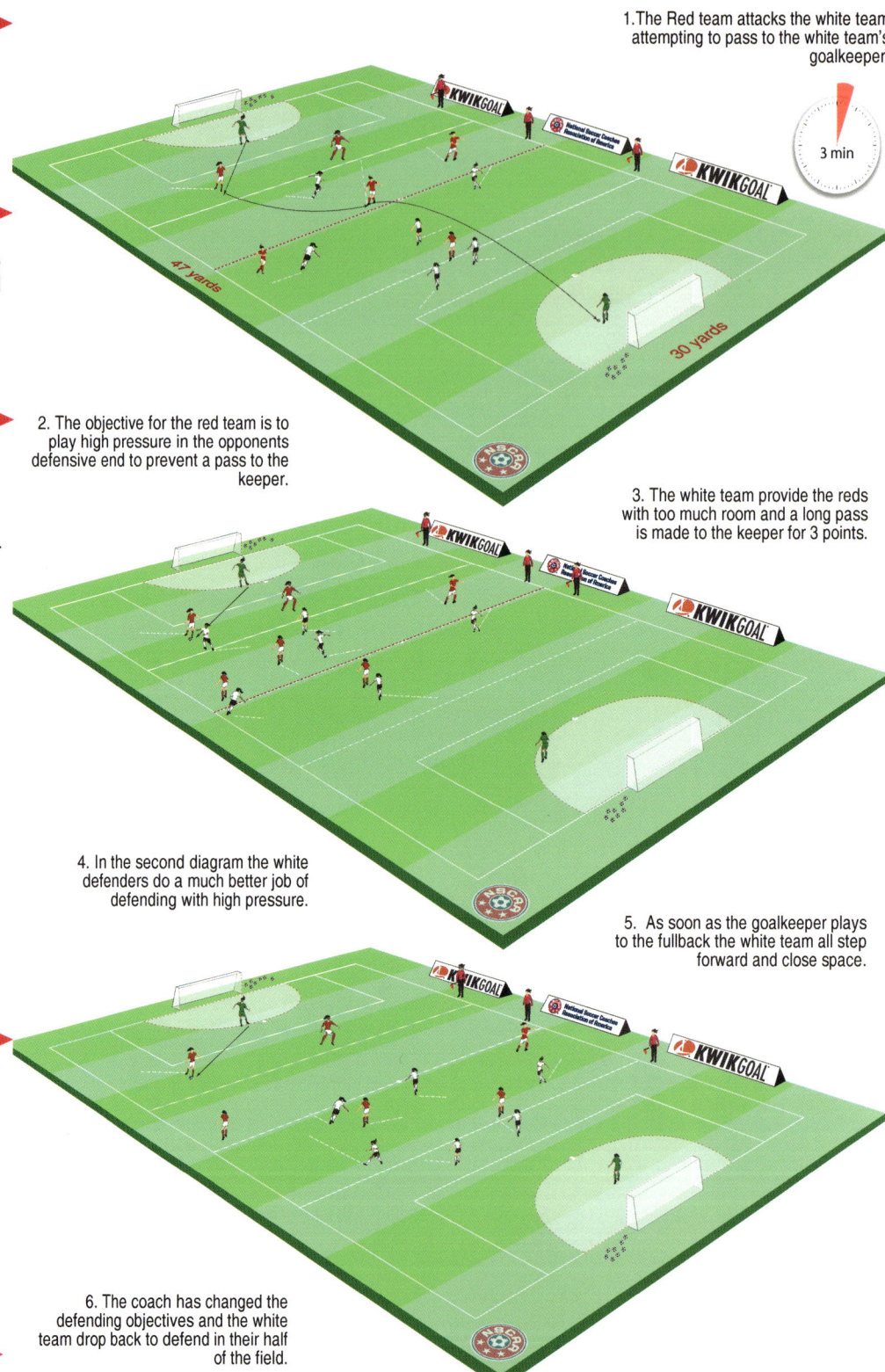

1. The Red team attacks the white team attempting to pass to the white team's goalkeeper.

2. The objective for the red team is to play high pressure in the opponents defensive end to prevent a pass to the keeper.

3. The white team provide the reds with too much room and a long pass is made to the keeper for 3 points.

4. In the second diagram the white defenders do a much better job of defending with high pressure.

5. As soon as the goalkeeper plays to the fullback the white team all step forward and close space.

6. The coach has changed the defending objectives and the white team drop back to defend in their half of the field.

Stage/s of development covered by activity
Stages 2, 3, 4 and 5 - 6-18 year old players.

Development themes and competencies
Top 3 Themes: Individual and pairs defending, when to press and when to hold and communication.
Top 3 Competencies: Defending pressure, defending cover and defending recovery.

4v3 TO 5v5 DEFENDING IN SMALL GROUPS - FUNCTIONAL

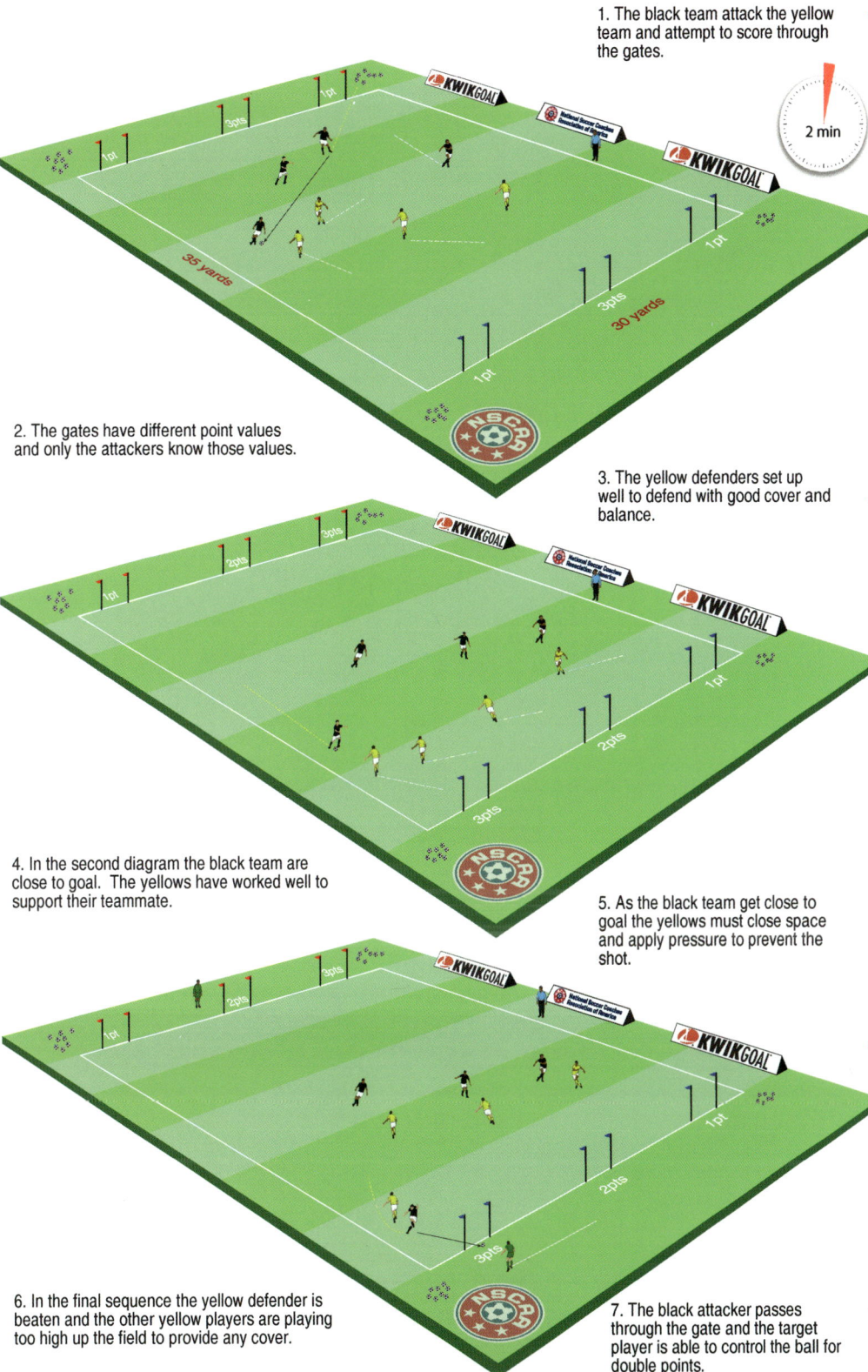

1. The black team attack the yellow team and attempt to score through the gates.

2. The gates have different point values and only the attackers know those values.

3. The yellow defenders set up well to defend with good cover and balance.

4. In the second diagram the black team are close to goal. The yellows have worked well to support their teammate.

5. As the black team get close to goal the yellows must close space and apply pressure to prevent the shot.

6. In the final sequence the yellow defender is beaten and the other yellow players are playing too high up the field to provide any cover.

7. The black attacker passes through the gate and the target player is able to control the ball for double points.

Why use it?

A common defensive shape for a 7v7 is to have 3 defenders - left, right and central, and a holding midfield player. This activity helps the 4 players to work together as a defensive unit, trading roles as the first (pressure), second (cover) and third/fourth (balance) defenders.

Set up

The set up is a 35x30 yards area with 3 flag goals on each end line. The goals are approximately 3 yards wide and each goal is awarded a different points value. Play 4v4 in the main area. A supply of balls are placed in each corner of the field to allow the players to restart the game continuously. The coach observes from the sideline.

How to play

The focus is on defending as a unit and adjusting the defensive shape to counter the attack. As the ball moves from one player to the next the defenders must adjust their positions and trade roles as the pressure, cover and balance defenders. If the defenders win possession of the ball they can counter attack. The coach should inform the teams the value of scoring in the opponents goals, but this should not be shared with the opponents. At the end of the game the players can reveal how many points they scored and which goals were worth 1,2 or 3 points. Play 8 intervals each lasting 2 minutes. Intervals 1-4 dribble or pass through the gates to score. Intervals 5-8 add a player/keeper behind the end line - if the player can control the ball that is played through the gates the points value is doubled.

Coaching notes

Coaching Objectives: Work with the players to adapt the shape of the defense based on the position of the ball and the opponents.
Coaching Tip: To help players with positioning and decision-making the coach may wish to freeze play, step onto the field, move players around, rehearse and then play live.

How to modify

Less Challenging: Reduce the size of the field so the defenders have less ground to cover.
More Challenging: Impose a time and/or touch restriction on the attackers. This condition will add urgency to the attack and will require more intense effort from the defenders.

Stage/s of development covered by activity

Stages 3, 4 and 5 - 9-18 year old players.

Development themes and competencies

Top 3 Themes: Individual, pairs and small group defending, transition and communication.
Top 3 Competencies: Defending pressure, defending cover and defending balance.

6v7 DEFENDING IN SMALL GROUPS - PHASE

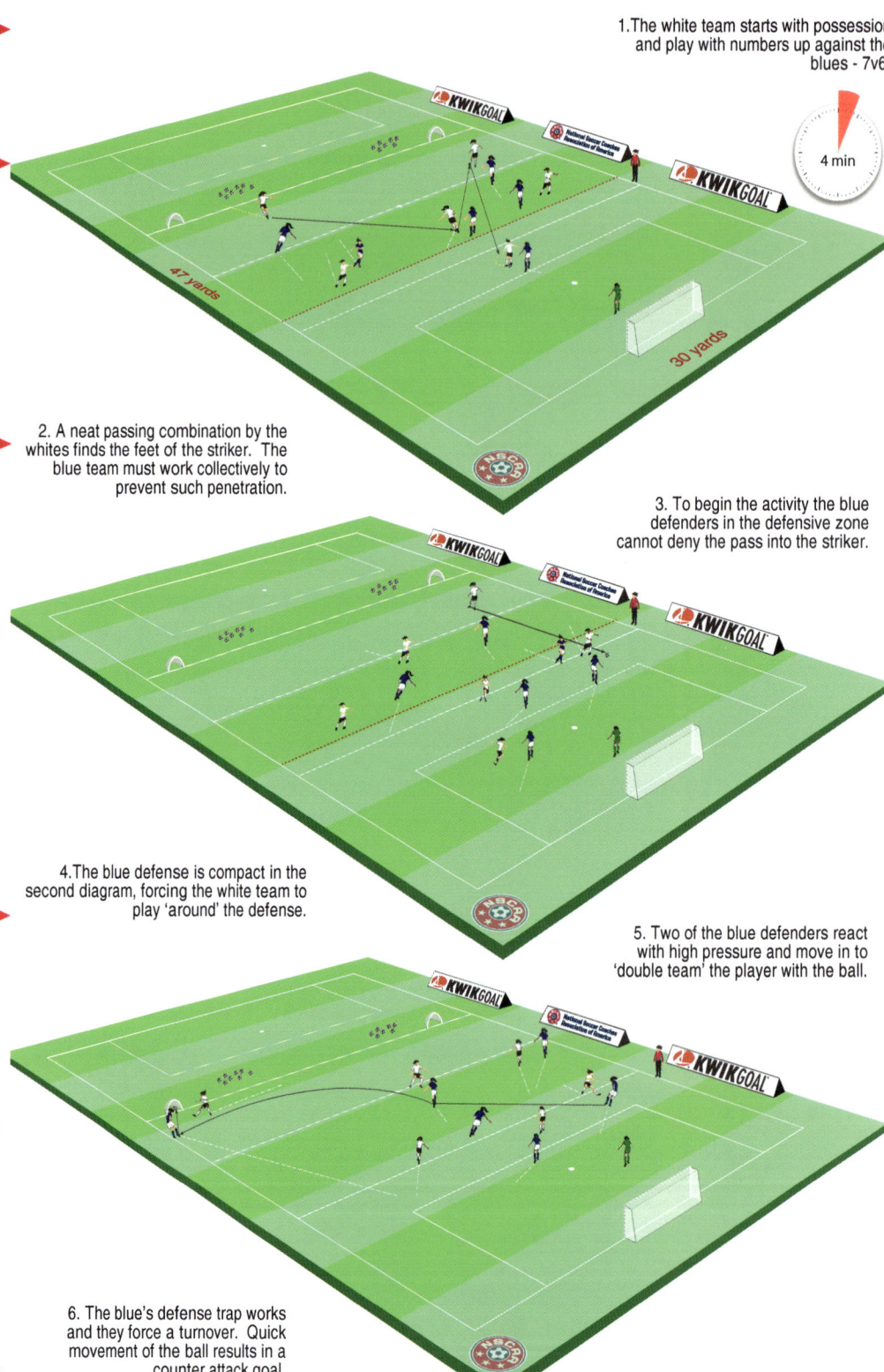

Why use it?
This activity builds on the previous activity and the theme of defending in units - pressure, cover and balance.

Set up
The set is approximately two-thirds of a 7v7 field with an appropriate size goal at one end and 2 mini goals on the other end line. The field is separated into two zones. Play 6v7 - a goalkeeper and defender against 1 attacker in the defensive zone and 5 attackers against 5 defenders in the attacking zone. The coach observes from the sideline.

How to play
The primary objectives for the defending team is to prevent the attacking team from entering the defending zone, to win possession and then counter attack to score in one of the mini goals. The attackers must attempt to get the ball to the striker in the defensive end and then 2 players can support to create a 3v2. To begin, the two defenders must allow the striker to receive the ball if the attacking team is able to get a pass through. Play 4 intervals each lasting 4 minutes. Intervals 1-2 allow 2 attackers to join the attack if a ball is played to the striker. Intervals 3-4 remove all the restrictions and let the defenders deny a pass played to the striker.

Coaching notes
Coaching Objectives: Communication between the defenders is key. The defensive shape should change based on the location of the ball. When the ball is central one defender applies pressure and 2 defenders cover to create a compact triangle. When the ball is wide one defender presses, the 2nd defender covers and 3rd defender offers balance - hips open, able to see both ball and far side defenders.
Coaching Tip: Patience must be taught to defenders in this numbers down activity. Defenders need to know that sometimes they don't have to win the ball immediately to be successful.

How to modify
Less Challenging: Reduce the size of the field. Allow the defenders to deny the pass into the striker.
More Challenging: Reduce the number of defenders.

1. The white team starts with possession and play with numbers up against the blues - 7v6.

2. A neat passing combination by the whites finds the feet of the striker. The blue team must work collectively to prevent such penetration.

3. To begin the activity the blue defenders in the defensive zone cannot deny the pass into the striker.

4. The blue defense is compact in the second diagram, forcing the white team to play 'around' the defense.

5. Two of the blue defenders react with high pressure and move in to 'double team' the player with the ball.

6. The blue's defense trap works and they force a turnover. Quick movement of the ball results in a counter attack goal.

Stage/s of development covered by activity
Stages 3, 4 and 5 - 9-18 year old players.

Development themes and competencies
Top 3 Themes: Individual, pairs and small group defending, transition and communication.
Top 3 Competencies: Defending pressure, defending cover and defending balance.

7v7 DEFENDING IN SMALL GROUPS - GAME

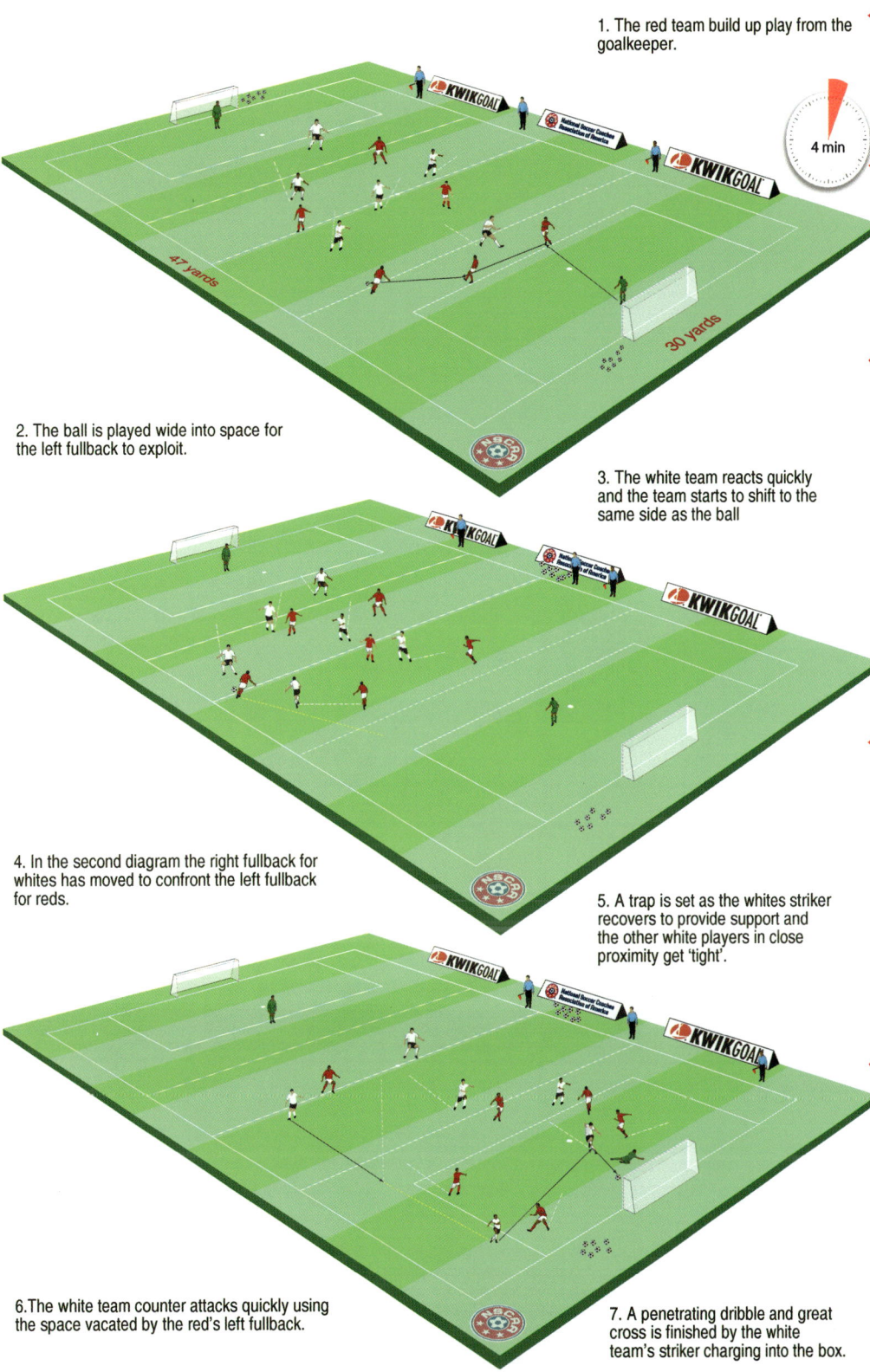

1. The red team build up play from the goalkeeper.

2. The ball is played wide into space for the left fullback to exploit.

3. The white team reacts quickly and the team starts to shift to the same side as the ball

4. In the second diagram the right fullback for whites has moved to confront the left fullback for reds.

5. A trap is set as the whites striker recovers to provide support and the other white players in close proximity get 'tight'.

6. The white team counter attacks quickly using the space vacated by the red's left fullback.

7. A penetrating dribble and great cross is finished by the white team's striker charging into the box.

Why use it?
This game like activity provides the coach with an opportunity to see if learning objectives from the previous activities can be applied in a 7v7 game setting.

4 min

Set up
The set up is full 7v7 field with an appropriate size goal at both ends. The coach observes from the sideline and is supported by 2 assistants monitoring offside.

How to play
The coach can set a variety of different objectives for the attacking and defending teams. Set up the formations and team shape to support the defensive objectives - i.e. high/low press, prevent attacks through the middle or around the edge etc. All restarts are from the goalkeepers. If the defense forces and turnover, the team must keep possession or the opponent wins a free kick. When they win the ball the defenders keep possession, stretch the opponent, offer opportunities to keep possession and penetrate to score.

Coaching notes
Coaching Objectives: Focus on whether or not the defense can read the appropriate cues and win possession. If the defender closest to the ball can arrive to apply pressure on or before the receiver's first touch the team should press hard. The second and third defenders must move close attacking options, mark opponents and 'squeeze' the game.
Coaching Tip: Use this activity to imprint a style of defensive shape with your team.

How to modify
Less Challenging: Attackers must take more than 2 touches to slow down the play. This will enable the defenders to get into position before the ball is passed again. Making the area smaller and more compact will also help the defenders, as the attackers will have less space to pass..
More Challenging: Team in possession has a maximum of 2 touches. This speeds up the play and less time for defenders to get into a good defensive shape. Also the coach can manipulate the attacking team to play long balls over the top to try to expose the weak side and defenders caught 'ball watching'.

Stage/s of development covered by activity
Stages 3, 4 and 5 - 9-18 year old players.

Development themes and competencies
Top 3 Themes: Individual, pairs and small group defending, transition and communication.
Top 3 Competencies: Defending pressure, defending cover and defending balance.

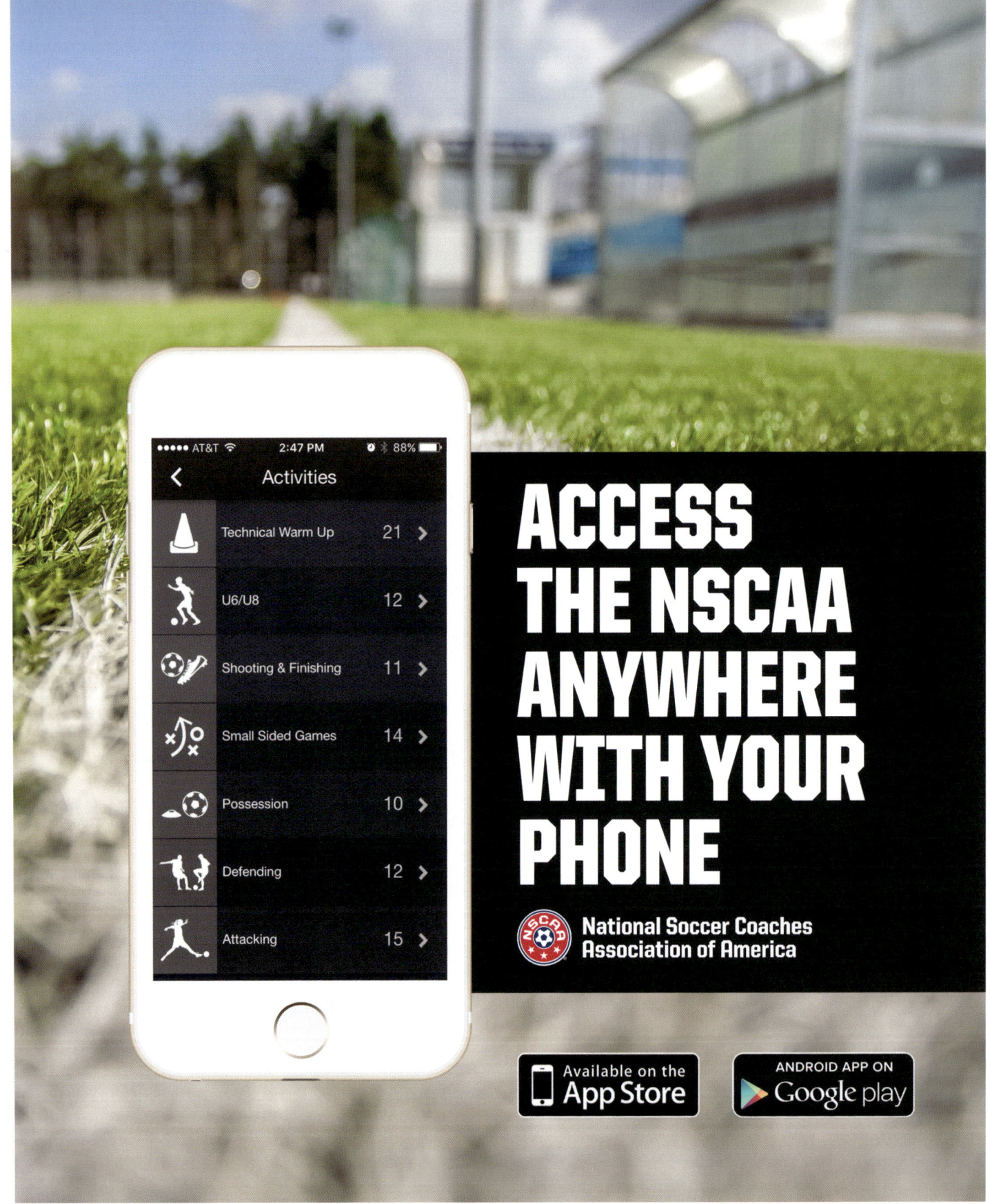

9v9 FORMATIONS - 1-4-3-1

Attacking Shape

Features of this shape:
A very popular formation with coaches preparing players for 11v11.
With all teammates playing in central positions, the fullbacks are encouraged to attack into the wide channels.
The central defenders and attacking midfield players form triangles centrally with the defending midfield player.
The lone striker must be proficient in retaining possession and linking with the 2 central attacking midfield players.

Defending Shape

Features of this shape:
Two central defenders are committed full-time to defending and must stay compact centrally.
The fullbacks must quickly recover from their attacking responsibilities. When the ball is wide the fullback nearest the ball applies pressure and the fullback on the opposite side balances the back 4.
Midfield players prevent penetration through the middle and down the seams between central defenders.

9v9 FORMATIONS - 1-2-3-3

Attacking Shape

Features of this shape:
An attacking formation with 3 central midfield players, 2 wingers and 1 striker.
The team is set up quite narrow with the width provided in the attacking third of the field. Quick transition is essential and defenders and midfield players should aim to play into the space behind the defense and wide.
The central striker should keep the opponent's central defenders busy to isolate the fullbacks 1v1.

Defending Shape

Features of this shape:
The central defenders and central midfield players form a defensive 'box' in front of goal.
The attacking midfield player must recover to the middle, allowing the defending midfield players to move laterally and apply pressure in wide positions.
Two wingers are expected to drop back behind the ball to form a solid line of 5 midfield in front of the defense.

9v9 FORMATIONS - 1-2-4-2

Attacking Shape

Features of this shape:
The mid-field and attacking lines are closely related to an 11v11 formation 1-4-4-2.
Width is provided by the right and left midfield players and the coach can play with the central players side by side or staggered with a defensive and attacking shape.
Two strikers work close together and are more often than not staggered - a main target with a 'withdrawn striker'.

Defending Shape

Features of this shape:
The central defenders and the defensive midfield player form a compact triangle at the top of the penalty box.
The wide midfield players tuck in towards the center of the field and form a defensive line of 3 with the attacking midfield player.
The two strikers work the left and right sides of the field and work in partnership with the wide midfield players.

9v9 CREATING SPACE IN THE FINAL THIRD 1

Why use it?

This 9v9 game related activity provides the coach with an opportunity to work on off the ball movement to create space in the final third of the field. Creating space with movement off the ball is certainly a challenging topic when working with young players and will take regular repetition and reinforcement to develop proficiency. Strikers initially move away from the ball and then make penetrating runs between and behind the defenders.

Set up

2 teams play on a full 9v9 field - 75x47 yards in size. To begin there are two games running concurrently at each end of the field. Each half is subdivided to create 2 zones. In each end the attacking team starts with 2 unopposed midfield players in the zone closest to the halfway line and in the attacking zone play 3v2 in favor of the attacking team. A server for the attacking team starts the activity on the sideline and starts the activity when all players are in a ready position. The coach stands to one side to observe both games.

How to play

The objective is to work with the front three forward players to create space in the final third. The servers initiate each attack passing to one of the midfield players. When a midfield player has the ball wide, the attacking players should make runs away from the player with the ball. This coordinated movement will either create space for the midfield player to penetrate with a dribble, or isolate a single striker 1v1 against a defender. The defenders cannot leave the end zone to begin. Progress to 3v3 in each end zone and 2v2 in the central zone using 1 ball. Play until 3 goals have been scored or in 5 minute intervals.

Coaching notes

Coaching Objectives: Help players to recognize visual cues to create space.
Coaching Tips: Be prepared to choreograph some designed movements and combination plays.

How to modify

Less Challenging: Remove defenders and work through some pattern play. Then add in 'passive' defenders.
More Challenging: Add more defenders to both zones, remove the zones and play 9v9 without restrictions.

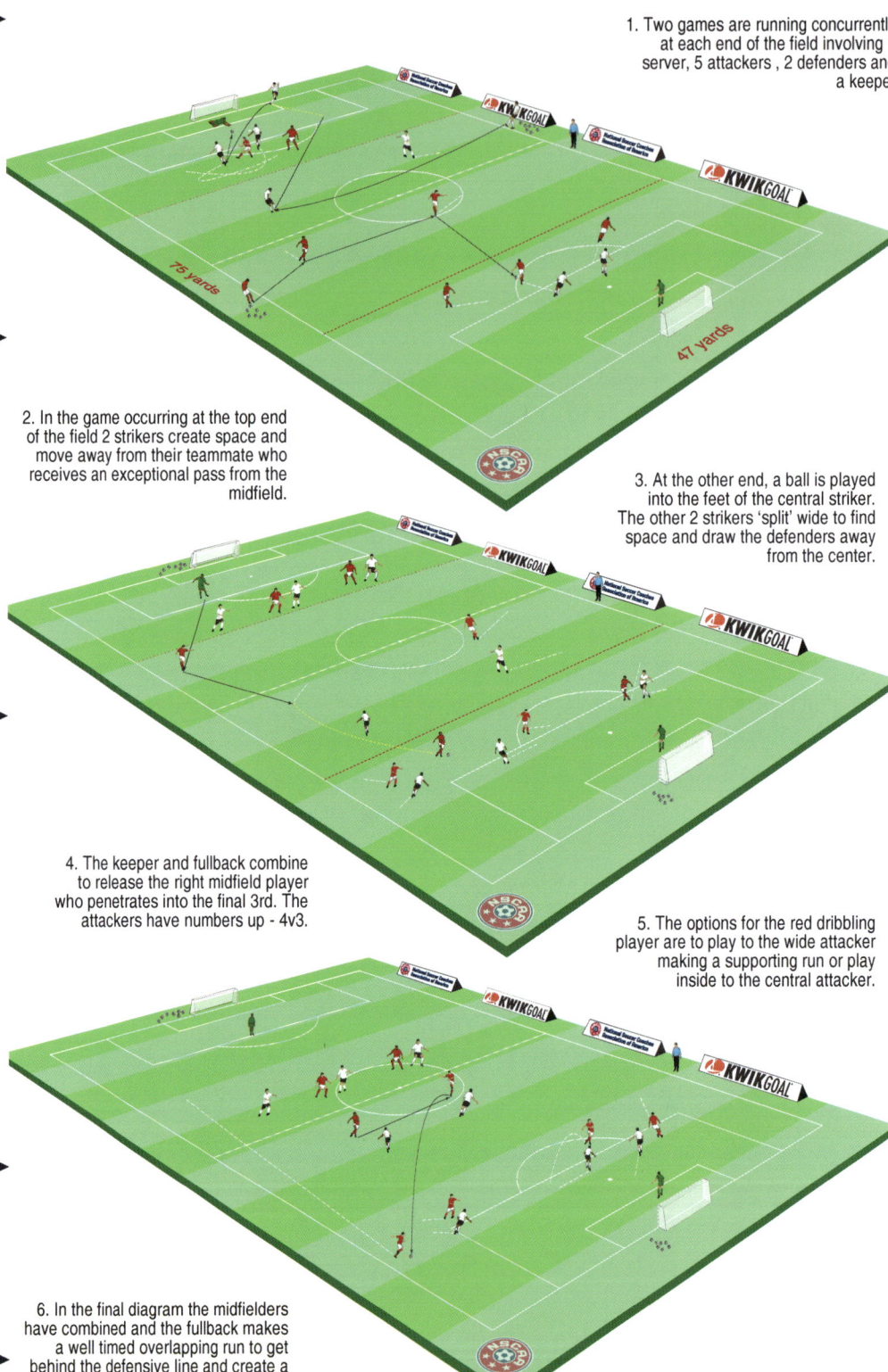

1. Two games are running concurrently at each end of the field involving 1 server, 5 attackers, 2 defenders and a keeper

2. In the game occurring at the top end of the field 2 strikers create space and move away from their teammate who receives an exceptional pass from the midfield.

3. At the other end, a ball is played into the feet of the central striker. The other 2 strikers 'split' wide to find space and draw the defenders away from the center.

4. The keeper and fullback combine to release the right midfield player who penetrates into the final 3rd. The attackers have numbers up - 4v3.

5. The options for the red dribbling player are to play to the wide attacker making a supporting run or play inside to the central attacker.

6. In the final diagram the midfielders have combined and the fullback makes a well timed overlapping run to get behind the defensive line and create a scoring opportunity.

Stage/s of development covered by activity

Stages 4 & 5 - 12-18 year old players.

Development themes and competencies

Top 3 Themes: Passing, creating space as an individual and team, and support.

Top 3 Competencies: Passing over short to medium distances, attacking as a unit of the team and communication.

9V9 CREATING SPACE IN THE FINAL THIRD 2

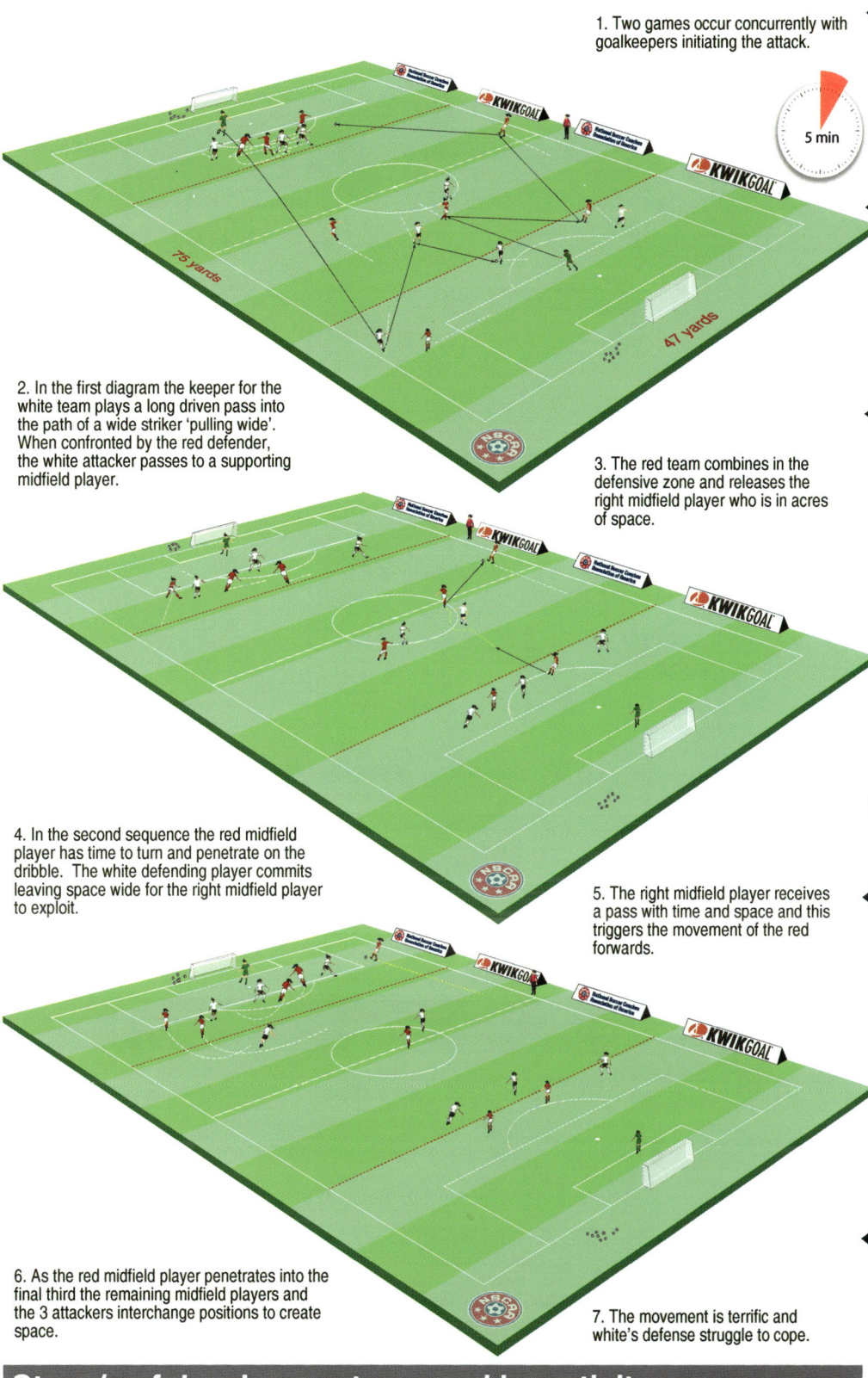

1. Two games occur concurrently with goalkeepers initiating the attack.

2. In the first diagram the keeper for the white team plays a long driven pass into the path of a wide striker 'pulling wide'. When confronted by the red defender, the white attacker passes to a supporting midfield player.

3. The red team combines in the defensive zone and releases the right midfield player who is in acres of space.

4. In the second sequence the red midfield player has time to turn and penetrate on the dribble. The white defending player commits leaving space wide for the right midfield player to exploit.

5. The right midfield player receives a pass with time and space and this triggers the movement of the red forwards.

6. As the red midfield player penetrates into the final third the remaining midfield players and the 3 attackers interchange positions to create space.

7. The movement is terrific and white's defense struggle to cope.

Why use it?
Continuing the theme of creating space, this activity provides the coach with opportunities to work with the midfield and forward players. With repetition the players will learn to identify visual cues and will respond with complementary movements.

Set up
2 teams play on a full 9v9 field - 75x47 yards in size. The field is subdivided into 3 zones. To begin there are two games running concurrently each initiated by the goalkeeper. The coach stands on the sideline to observe and coach.

How to play
The objective is to work with the front three forward and midfield players to create space in the middle and final thirds of the field. In the first sequence the goalkeeper initiates the attack with a pass or throw to a teammate. The attacking players are allowed to move freely, but the defenders must remain in the zone they started or quickly recover to their zone once an attack has broken down. The team the coach will work with first should be set up in a 1-2-3-3 formation and the opponent in a 1-3-2-3. The attacking team should attempt to create a numbers up situation in each zone. When possession is lost the players return to their original starting zone. Play until 3 goals have been scored or in 5 minute intervals.

Coaching notes
Coaching Objectives: At first encourage the attacking team to attack from wide positions so the visual cues are clear for the forwards. Movements should be away from the ball carrier to create space in dangerous positions and then cut back towards the ball.
Coaching Tips: Insist the passing is crisp and realistic to the game. Creating movement restrictions on players can sometimes result in players losing concentration and playing at half pace.

How to modify
Less Challenging: Remove defenders and work through some pattern plays. Add in 'passive' defenders and reduce the length of the field to start attacks closer to goal.
More Challenging: Remove the zones and play 9v9 without restrictions.

Stage/s of development covered by activity
Stages 4 & 5 - 12-18 year old players.

Development themes and competencies
Top 3 Themes: Passing, creating space as an individual and team, and support.
Top 3 Competencies: Passing over short to medium distances, attacking as a unit of the team and communication.

CREATING SPACE IN 9v9 GAME

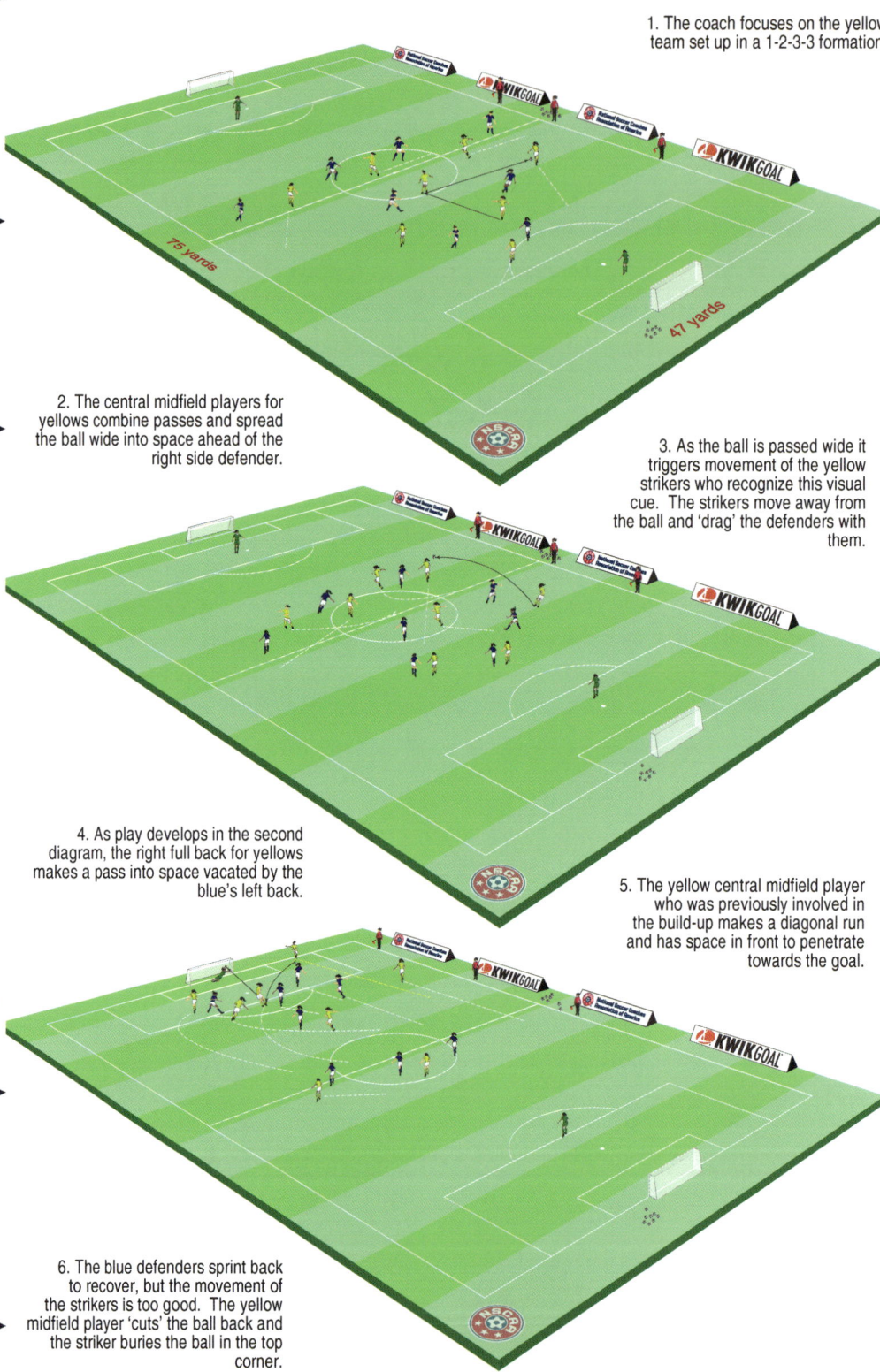

Why use it?
The final game activity is a great way to determine how much the players have learned during the technical, functional and phase of play sessions. The emphasis and focus for the coach is movement of players in the final third of the field to create individual and team space.

Set up
The set up is a full 9v9 field with an appropriate size goal at both ends. The coach observes from the sideline and is supported by 2 assistants monitoring offside. Both teams have a full complement of players - 9v9 - to start.

How to play
Begin by setting up the team you are going to coach in an attacking formation -1-2-3-3. The opponent should be set up in a 1-4-2-2 formation. Commence with a pass/throw from the goalkeeper playing for the team you are coaching. Once the ball enters the field, play normal rules. The objective for the attacking team is to attack the opponent down either flank and for the strikers and attacking midfield players to work on movement patterns to find space. Initially 3 players on the defending team are prevented from recovering into their defensive half. This condition should create a numerical overload in attack. Encourage the strikers to switch positions as the attack develops, making it difficult for the defenders to 'mark' the attackers. Use a points system to emphasize attacking with pace. A goal scored within 8 seconds is worth 5 points and a goal scored in 9 or more seconds is worth 1 point. Play until the attacking team has scored 15 points or for 8 minutes per interval. Play a total of 3 intervals.

Coaching notes
Coaching Objectives: Help players to recognize the correct timing of movements to create space for an individual and/or a teammate.
Coaching Tips: Be prepared to choreograph some designed movements and combination plays.

How to modify
Less Challenging: Reduce the number of defenders and then add them back gradually.
More Challenging: Restrict the number of touches allowed by the attacking players. Allow all the defenders to recover over the halfway line.

1. The coach focuses on the yellow team set up in a 1-2-3-3 formation.

2. The central midfield players for yellows combine passes and spread the ball wide into space ahead of the right side defender.

3. As the ball is passed wide it triggers movement of the yellow strikers who recognize this visual cue. The strikers move away from the ball and 'drag' the defenders with them.

4. As play develops in the second diagram, the right full back for yellows makes a pass into space vacated by the blue's left back.

5. The yellow central midfield player who was previously involved in the build-up makes a diagonal run and has space in front to penetrate towards the goal.

6. The blue defenders sprint back to recover, but the movement of the strikers is too good. The yellow midfield player 'cuts' the ball back and the striker buries the ball in the top corner.

Stage/s of development covered by activity
Stages 4 & 5 - 12-18 year old players.

Development themes and competencies
Top 3 Themes: Passing, creating space as an individual and team, and support.
Top 3 Competencies: Passing over short to medium distances, attacking as a unit of the team and communication.

DEFENSIVE ORGANIZATION BACK 4

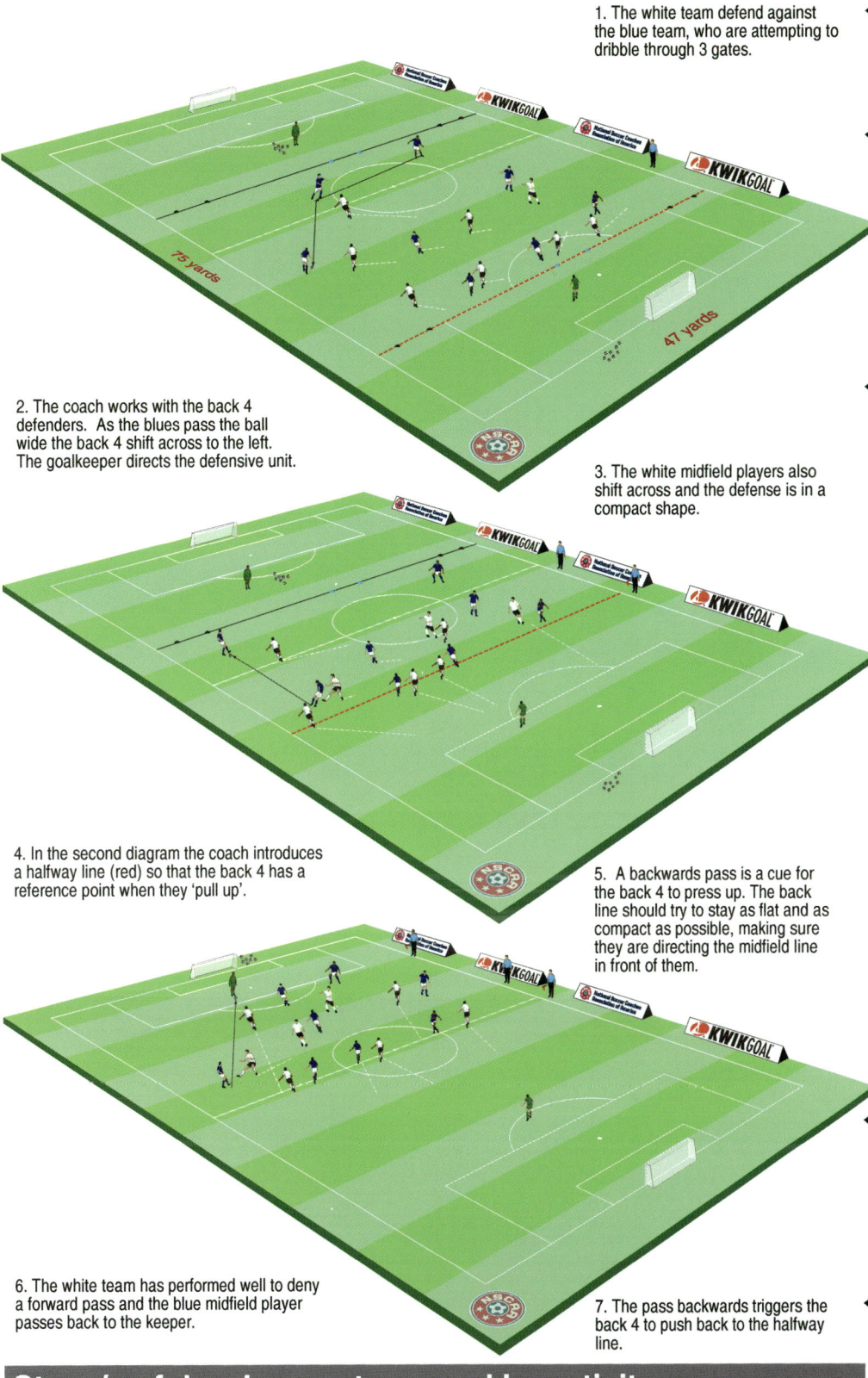

1. The white team defend against the blue team, who are attempting to dribble through 3 gates.

2. The coach works with the back 4 defenders. As the blues pass the ball wide the back 4 shift across to the left. The goalkeeper directs the defensive unit.

3. The white midfield players also shift across and the defense is in a compact shape.

4. In the second diagram the coach introduces a halfway line (red) so that the back 4 has a reference point when they 'pull up'.

5. A backwards pass is a cue for the back 4 to press up. The back line should try to stay as flat and as compact as possible, making sure they are directing the midfield line in front of them.

6. The white team has performed well to deny a forward pass and the blue midfield player passes back to the keeper.

7. The pass backwards triggers the back 4 to push back to the halfway line.

Why use it?

This activity provides the coach with an opportunity to work with the organization of the back 4 defenders.

Set up

2 teams play on three quarters of a 9v9 field. A defensive zone is marked across the top of the penalty box and 3 gate goals are created at both ends of the field. Play 9v9 with a goalkeeper for each team standing in the space behind each end line. The coach stands on the sideline to observe and instruct.

How to play

The defensive objective is to work on a sequence of scenarios with the back 4 defenders. As the ball is transferred by the attacking team to different parts of the field the defensive unit must shift. The goalkeeper is an important part of the defensive unit and has an ideal vantage point to help direct the movement of the back 4. The coach should focus on the team defending the full-size goal. Set up the team in a 1-4-3-1 formation and the opponents in a 1-2-3-3 formation. If the defenders win possession they attack the 3 gate goals and can score by passing the ball through. The attacking team also have 3 goals and must dribble through In the first sequence to score a point. In the first interval, the goalkeepers start as servers behind the end lines. The coach then removes the restraining line at the top of the box and the 'dribbling goals'. The offside law is now in effect so use the support of an assistant to monitor the offsides line. The attacking objective is to score in the full size goal. In the final interval the coach removes the 'passing goals' and the teams play on a full field. Play until one team scores 3 goals or in 5 minute intervals.

Coaching notes

Coaching Objectives: Work with players to trade roles - pressure, cover and balance.
Coaching Tips: Communication between the defenders is crucial to coordinate the movement of the defensive unit.

How to modify

Less Challenging: Reduce the size of the area.
More Challenging: Reduce the number of defenders

Stage/s of development covered by activity

Stages 4 & 5 - 12-18 year old players.

Development themes and competencies

Top 3 Themes: Defensive organization, pressure, cover and balance roles, counter attack.
Top 3 Competencies: Defending in pairs and small groups, positional play and communication.

DEFENSIVE ORGANIZATION MIDFIELD 3

Why use it?
This activity emphasizes the defensive responsibility of the midfield players and specifically recovery runs and organization of a midfield 3.

Set up
Played on a 9v9 field, a zone is marked from the halfway line 8 yards inside one half. At the other end place a full size goal. The coach observes from the sideline and is supported by 2 assistants monitoring offside.

How to play
The focus of this session is the defensive organization of the team defending the full size goal. Play starts from the goalkeeper, and the team defending the goal has to work the ball up into the zone adjacent to the halfway line. Once the team has the ball in the zone, the players have to make 3 consecutive passes for a point. The opponent must attempt to win possession and counter attack. As soon as the team turnover possession, the midfield 3 must make recovery runs to solidify the defense in front of the defenders.

Coaching notes
Coaching Objectives: Work with the midfield players on the recovery runs, shape of the defense, roles of pressure and cover and communication between the players.
Coaching Tips: Instead of stopping play or requiring the defenders to kick the ball out, provide both teams with an objective when the ball is won to add realism to the practice.

How to modify
Less Challenging: Reduce the number of attackers and then add them back gradually.
More Challenging: Delay the recover runs of one or more of the midfield players.

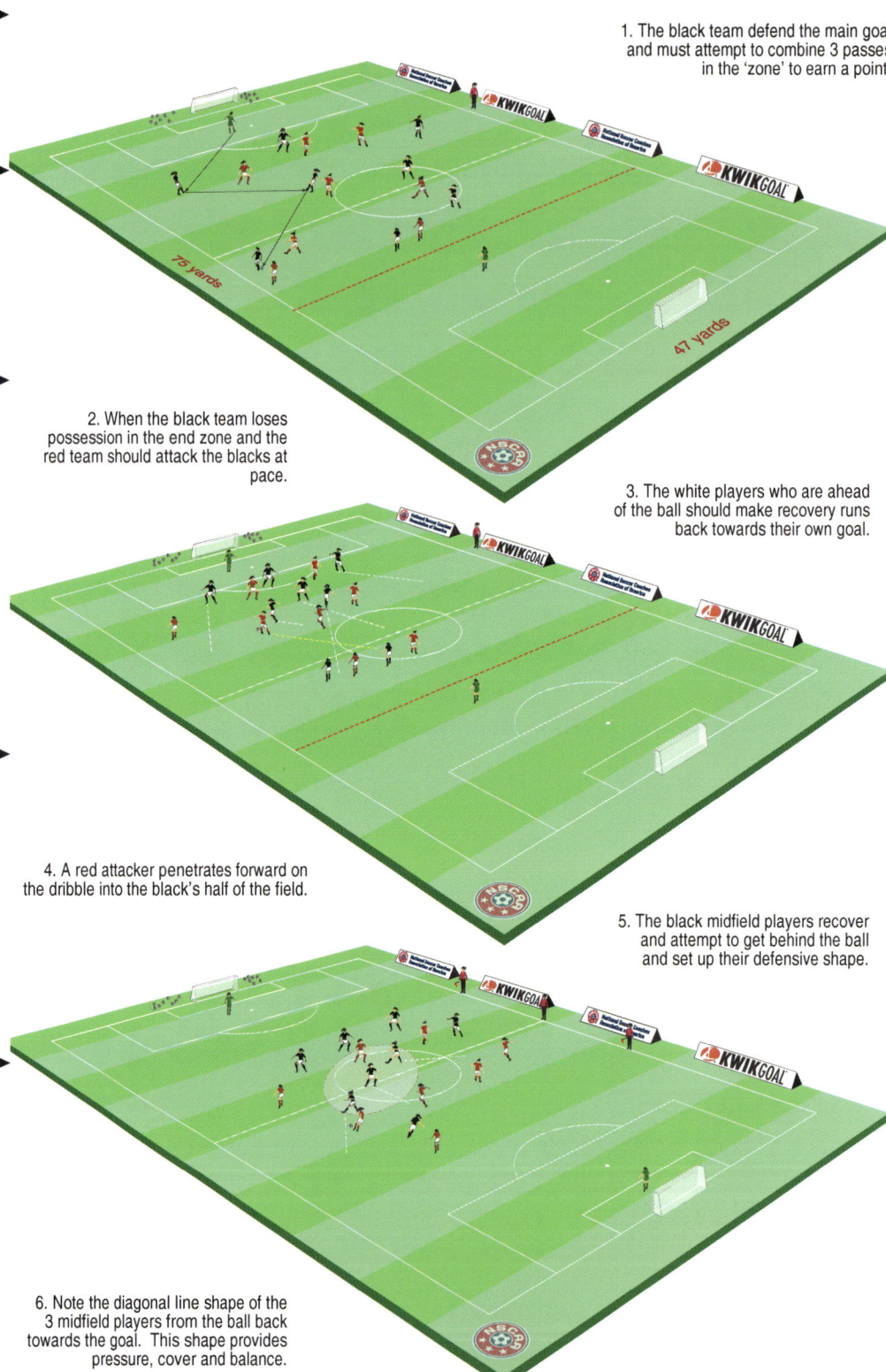

1. The black team defend the main goal and must attempt to combine 3 passes in the 'zone' to earn a point.

2. When the black team loses possession in the end zone and the red team should attack the blacks at pace.

3. The white players who are ahead of the ball should make recovery runs back towards their own goal.

4. A red attacker penetrates forward on the dribble into the black's half of the field.

5. The black midfield players recover and attempt to get behind the ball and set up their defensive shape.

6. Note the diagonal line shape of the 3 midfield players from the ball back towards the goal. This shape provides pressure, cover and balance.

Stage/s of development covered by activity
Stages 4 & 5 - 12-18 year old players.

Development themes and competencies
Top 3 Themes: Defensive organization, pressure, cover and balance roles, and counter attack.
Top 3 Competencies: Defending in pairs and small groups, positional play and communication.

DEFENSIVE ORGANIZATION HIGH PRESSURE

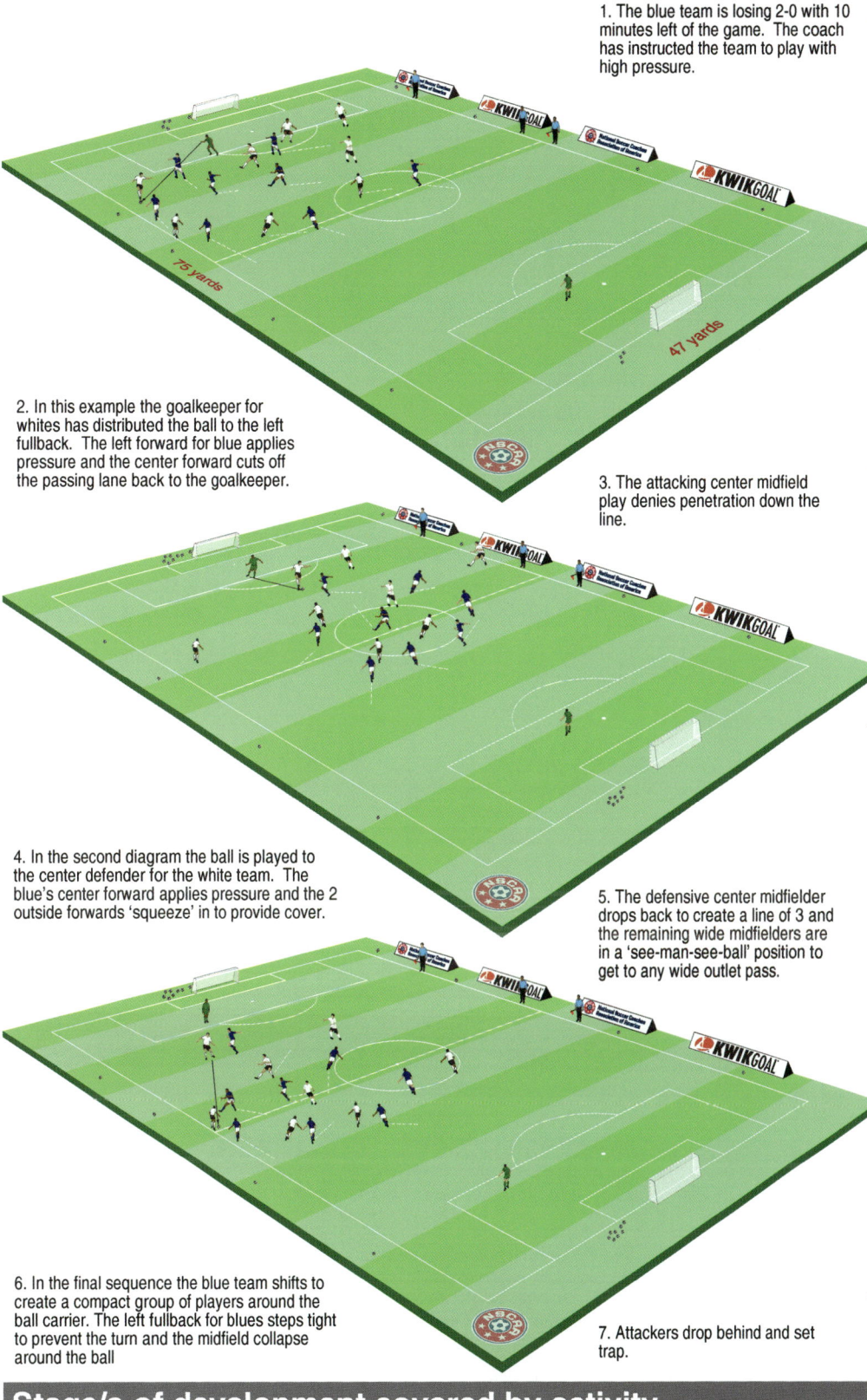

1. The blue team is losing 2-0 with 10 minutes left of the game. The coach has instructed the team to play with high pressure.

2. In this example the goalkeeper for whites has distributed the ball to the left fullback. The left forward for blue applies pressure and the center forward cuts off the passing lane back to the goalkeeper.

3. The attacking center midfield play denies penetration down the line.

4. In the second diagram the ball is played to the center defender for the white team. The blue's center forward applies pressure and the 2 outside forwards 'squeeze' in to provide cover.

5. The defensive center midfielder drops back to create a line of 3 and the remaining wide midfielders are in a 'see-man-see-ball' position to get to any wide outlet pass.

6. In the final sequence the blue team shifts to create a compact group of players around the ball carrier. The left fullback for blues steps tight to prevent the turn and the midfield collapse around the ball

7. Attackers drop behind and set trap.

Why use it?
This activity introduces a scenario occurring frequently in competitive games. Your team is trailing 2-0 with 10 minutes of regular time remaining and there is a heightened level of urgency for your team to win the ball back. Coordinated high pressure defense is required to force a turnover.

Set up
The set up is full 9v9 field with an appropriate size goal at both ends. The coach observes from the sideline and is supported by 2 assistants monitoring offside. Both teams have a full complement of players - 9v9 - to start.

How to play
With very little time remaining in the game, the coach instructs the team to play high pressure with the objective to force an immediate turnover. In the event that the team you are coaching loses the ball, introduce the 'Barcelona Rule' - your team must attempt to win back possession within 6 seconds of losing it.

Coaching notes
Coaching Objectives: When the team is 'out' of possession the defense must step into high gear and the nearest player must work tirelessly to close down the player with the ball. All other teammates are responsible to deny a pass and this is achieved with the 2-3 players nearest the ball collapsing the space around the ball carrier and getting close to their opponents.
Coaching Tips: Communication between the defenders is crucial to coordinate movement of the defensive unit. Recognizing an opportunity to play high pressure must involve the entire team and all players must know their responsibilities to provide pressure, cover and balance. Equally, the coach must restrain the young players from chasing all over the field in a disorganize manner. There is a fine balance between high intensity and thoughtless defending.

How to modify
Less Challenging: Place balls around the perimeter of the field to allow the attacking team to quickly restart. Require the attacking players to take at least 2 touches to allow the defenders a second or two extra time to close space.
More Challenging: Encourage the attacking team to play 1-2 touch.

Stage/s of development covered by activity
Stages 4 & 5 - 12-18 year old players.

Development themes and competencies
Top 3 Themes: Defensive organization, pressure, cover and balance roles, counter attack.
Top 3 Competencies: Defending as a team, high pressure defending and communication.

SWITCHING THE POINT OF ATTACK

Why use it?

The ability of a team to move the ball quickly from one side of the field to another is a tremendous advantage, particularly when faced with a well organized and resolute defense.

Set up

Played on a 9v9 field, use cones to create zone down both sides of the field. The cones should extend from the goal post to the halfway line (approximately 2 yards from the sideline. Only after an attacker has received or dribbled the ball into the wide zone can a defender enter the same space. The coach observes from the sideline and is supported by 2 assistants monitoring offside.

How to play

Play a regular game with only attackers permitted to enter the wide zones first. The objective for the attacking team is to move the ball at pace and attempt to pass the ball into the wide zone to exploit time and space. The central defenders and central midfield players are important in transitioning the ball from side to side. A goal can only be scored if the ball has 'visited' both wide zones consecutively. This condition forces the players to switch play.

Coaching notes

Coaching Objectives: Help the players to recognize when a switch of play is available. Cues such as a defense playing high pressure on one side of the field and an attacking overload developing on the 'weak-side', provide some indication that a switch of play may be possible.
Coaching Tips: In this instance the use of a wide zone keeps the defense relatively narrow and provides an opportunity for the attacking team to make a switch of play into an area permitting only the attacker.

How to modify

Less Challenging: Reduce the number of defenders and then add them back gradually. Also make the zones wider to force the defenders inside the field to free up more wide space.
More Challenging: Reduce the number of touches allowed for each player. Allow the defenders to enter the zones at the same time as the ball and attacker. The final progression is to allow players to go anywhere, but maintain the requirement of passing to both flanks consecutively before scoring.

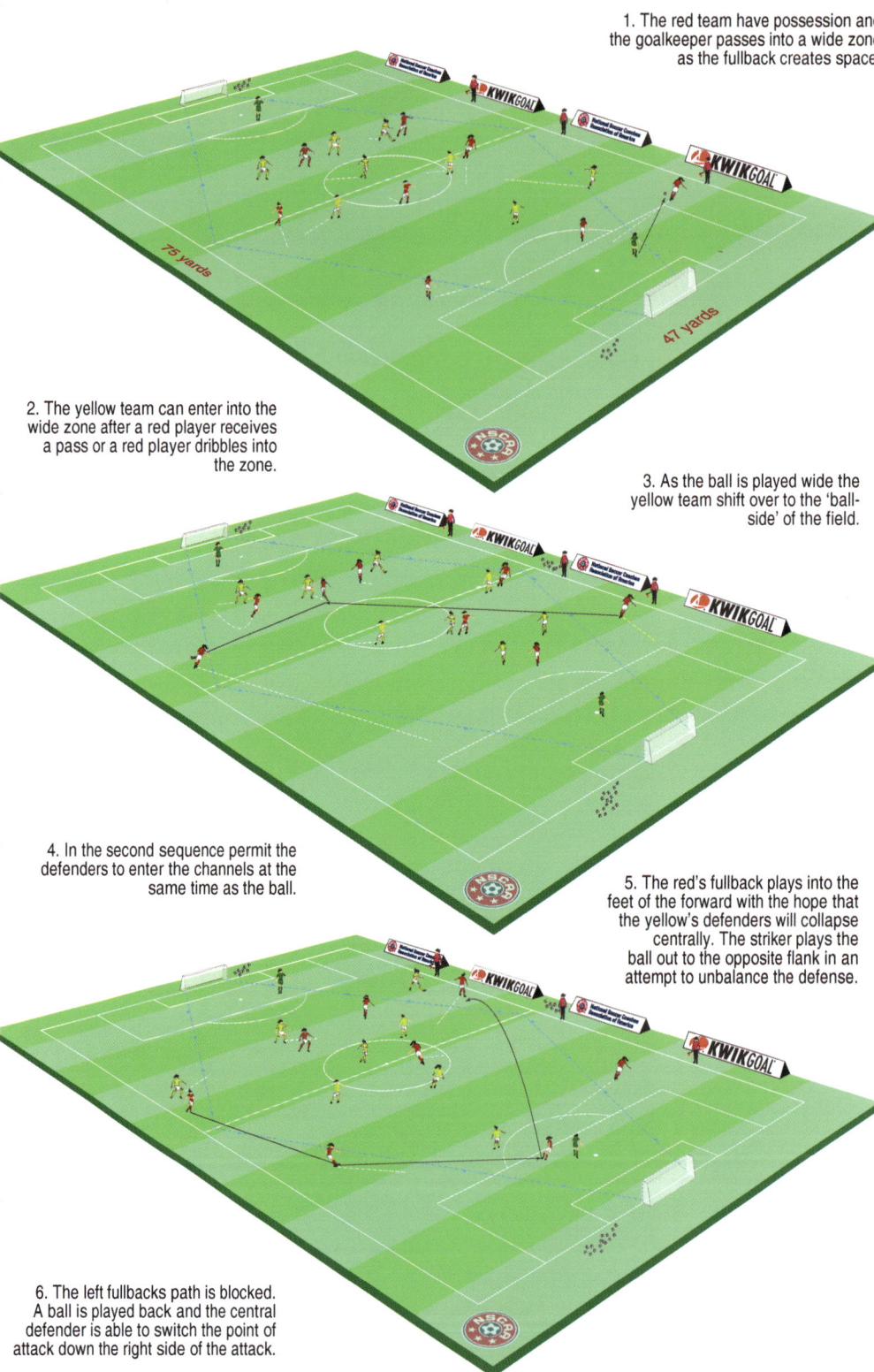

1. The red team have possession and the goalkeeper passes into a wide zone as the fullback creates space.

2. The yellow team can enter into the wide zone after a red player receives a pass or a red player dribbles into the zone.

3. As the ball is played wide the yellow team shift over to the 'ball-side' of the field.

4. In the second sequence permit the defenders to enter the channels at the same time as the ball.

5. The red's fullback plays into the feet of the forward with the hope that the yellow's defenders will collapse centrally. The striker plays the ball out to the opposite flank in an attempt to unbalance the defense.

6. The left fullbacks path is blocked. A ball is played back and the central defender is able to switch the point of attack down the right side of the attack.

Stage/s of development covered by activity

Stages 4 & 5 - 12-18 year old players.

Development themes and competencies

Top 3 Themes: Switching the point of attack, possession and creating space as a team.

Top 3 Competencies: Passing over medium and long distances, movement to create space and communication.

9V9 ATTACKING THE WEAK-SIDE

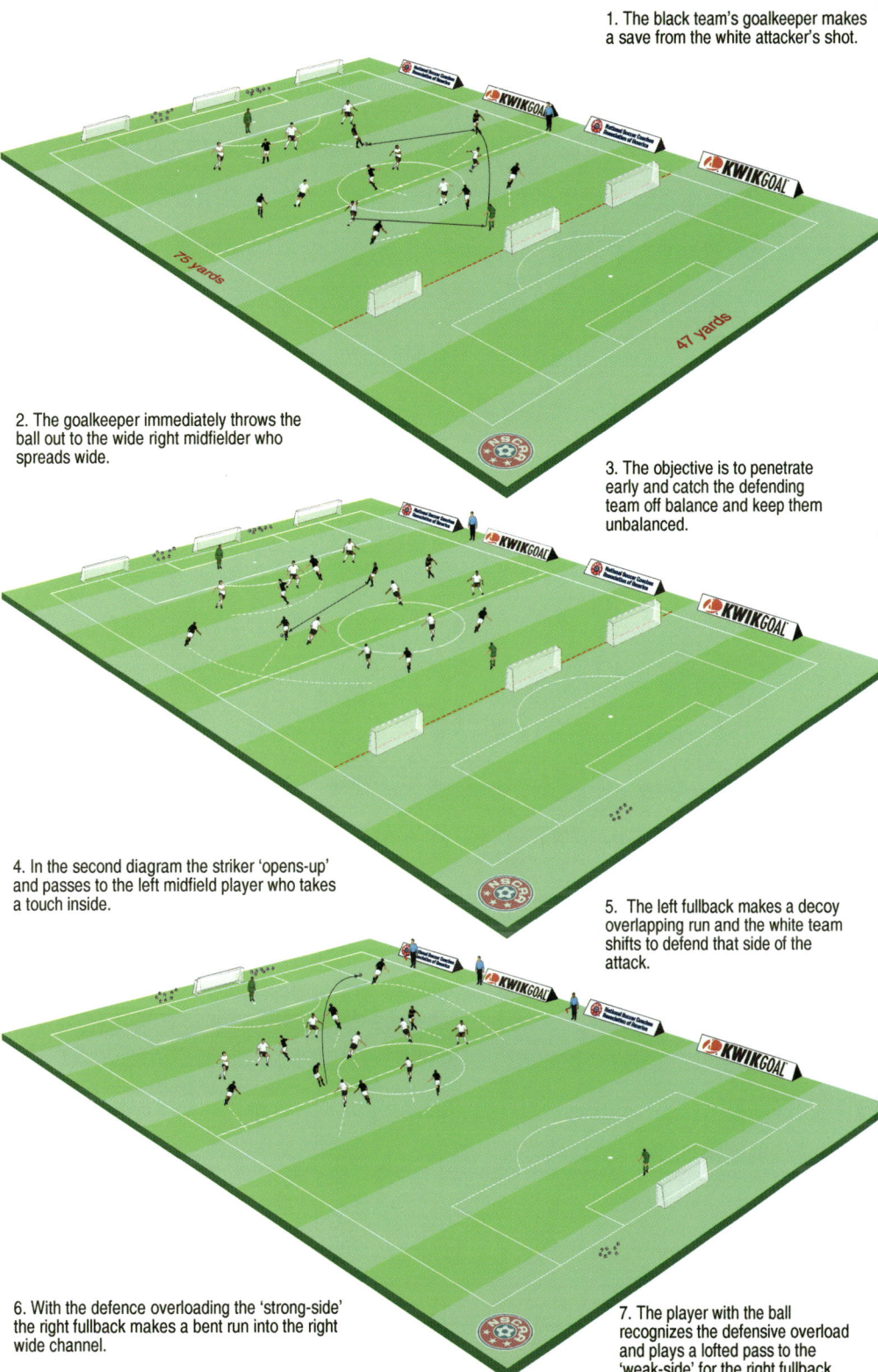

1. The black team's goalkeeper makes a save from the white attacker's shot.
2. The goalkeeper immediately throws the ball out to the wide right midfielder who spreads wide.
3. The objective is to penetrate early and catch the defending team off balance and keep them unbalanced.
4. In the second diagram the striker 'opens-up' and passes to the left midfield player who takes a touch inside.
5. The left fullback makes a decoy overlapping run and the white team shifts to defend that side of the attack.
6. With the defence overloading the 'strong-side' the right fullback makes a bent run into the right wide channel.
7. The player with the ball recognizes the defensive overload and plays a lofted pass to the 'weak-side' for the right fullback.

Why use it?
This 9v9 game related activity provides the coach with an opportunity to work on off the ball movement to create space in the wide channels. Players initially move towards the ball to open up the weak-side wide channel for the outside backs to exploit. This is an ideal activity if your team is having a problem getting around a packed defense or if you are constantly having to tell your flank players to stay wide.

Set up
2 teams play on three quarters of a 9v9 field. 3 goals are placed along the end line at both ends of the field. Play 9v9 with a goalkeeper for each team. The coach stands on the sideline to observe and instruct.

How to play
Play a regulation game with all FIFA rules applied. The attacking team the coach will be working with is set up in a 1-3-3-2 formation. The opposing team is set up in a 1-3-2-3 formation. There are 3 goals for each team to attack and the goalkeeper can move laterally to project all 3 goals. Encourage the attacking team to score in a goal unprotected by the goalkeeper. One point for a goal except for a one touch finish worth 3 points. It is important the opponent starts the attack as the coach will want the attacking team to commence from a compact defensive position. The objective is for the attacking team to spread wide quickly once the ball is turned over or the goalkeeper has made a save. If the defense is able to block the route to goal, the attackers should look to play early into the space on the 'weak-side' of the field.

Coaching notes
Coaching Objectives: The coach should attempt to develop some patterns of play in attack. Particular emphasis should be on forward and midfield players making runs away from the player with the ball and cutting back into dangerous areas vacated by creative movement of teammates.
Coaching Tip: The coach can control the tempo of the game by playing a ball to the opponent to take a shot on goal.

How to modify
Less Challenging: Make the defenders start the activity from behind the attackers goal.
More Challenging: Reduce the number of attackers if there are too many scoring opportunities.

Stage/s of development covered by activity
Stages 4 & 5 - 12-18 year old players.

Development themes and competencies
Top 3 Themes: Switching the point of attack, possession and creating space as a team.
Top 3 Competencies: Passing over medium and long distances, movement to create space and communication.

9V9 PATIENCE IN ATTACK

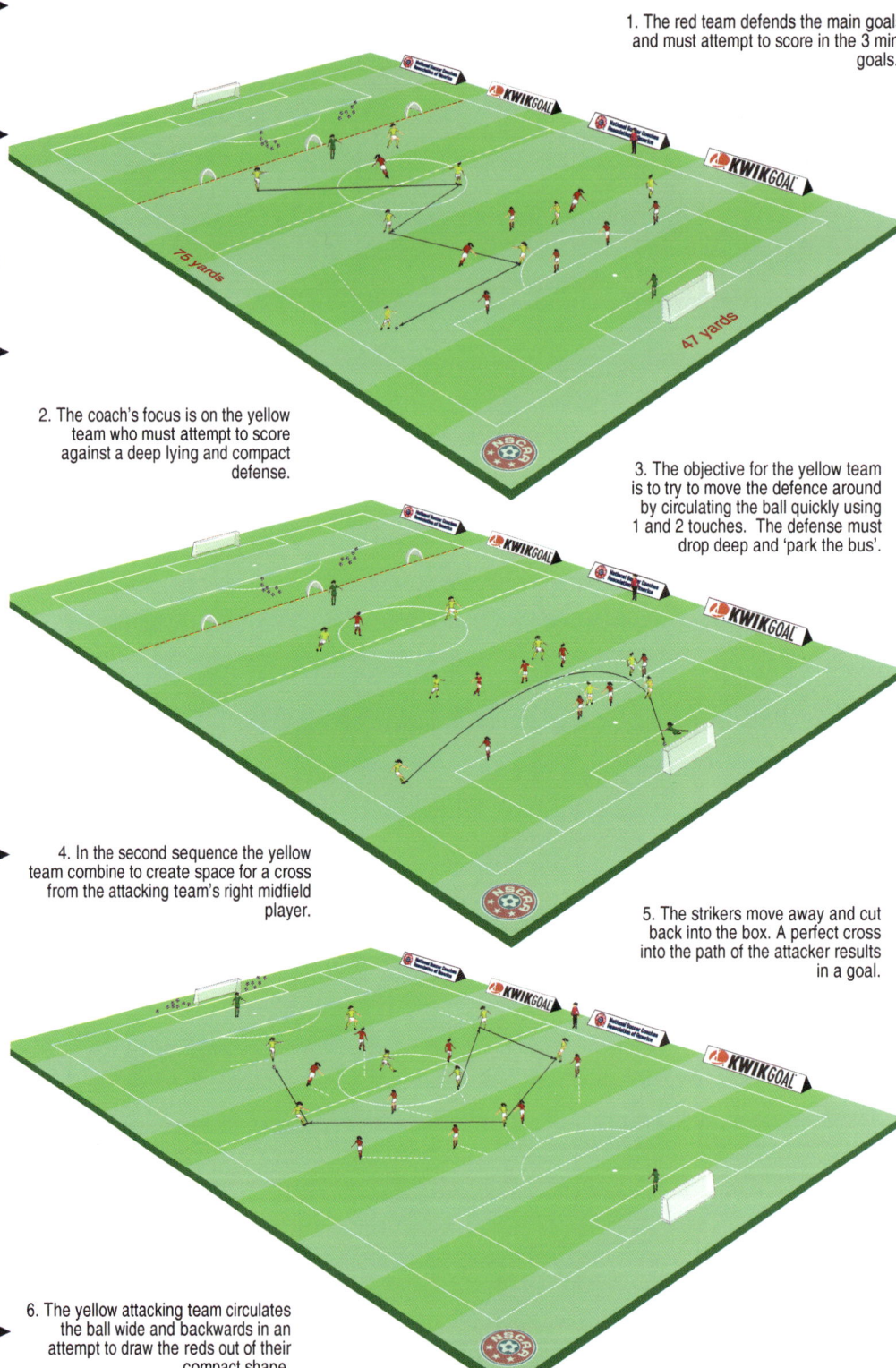

Why use it?
The coach can use this activity to break down a team that is defending deep in front of their own goal (parked the bus).

Set up
2 teams play on three quarters of a 9v9 field. At one end there is an appropriate size goal and at the other end are 3 mini goals. Play 9v9 with a goalkeeper for each team. The coach stands on the sideline to observe and instruct.

How to play
The coach is working with the team attacking the full goal and defending the mini goals. The attacking objective is to score against a deep lying and compact defense. This can be achieved a couple of ways. Firstly, the attacking team must be patient in their build-up and must attempt to move the defense laterally by exchanging passes quickly and with considerable movement of players along the forward line. A second strategy is to maintain possession away from goal in an attempt to draw the opponents towards the ball - a tactic that is more effective with youth players than a disciplined adult team. If the defenders win possession they must attempt to score in the 3 mini goals.

Coaching notes
Coaching Objectives: Work with the players to maintain possession and to probe the defense with movement and penetrative passing. A pass to an attackers feet may draw the surrounding players towards the ball, leaving space out wide to attack.

Coaching Tips: On occasion the best time to beat a deep lying defense is when it has possession of the ball. In order to have a chance of scoring the team must send some players forward and this temporarily weakens the compact defensive shape. If the opponent can win possession and counter at pace, the defenders may not be able to regain the defensive shape quickly enough.

How to modify
Less Challenging: Reduce the number of defenders.
More Challenging: Reduce the number of touches allowed for each player. Decrease the size of the area.

1. The red team defends the main goals and must attempt to score in the 3 mini goals..

2. The coach's focus is on the yellow team who must attempt to score against a deep lying and compact defense.

3. The objective for the yellow team is to try to move the defence around by circulating the ball quickly using 1 and 2 touches. The defense must drop deep and 'park the bus'.

4. In the second sequence the yellow team combine to create space for a cross from the attacking team's right midfield player.

5. The strikers move away and cut back into the box. A perfect cross into the path of the attacker results in a goal.

6. The yellow attacking team circulates the ball wide and backwards in an attempt to draw the reds out of their compact shape.

Stage/s of development covered by activity
Stages 4 & 5 - 12-18 year old players.

Development themes and competencies
Top 3 Themes: Switching the point of attack, possession and creating space as a team.

Top 3 Competencies: Passing over medium and long distances, movement to create space and communication.

4V3 TO 4V4 MIDFIELD PRESSURE AND COUNTER ATTACK

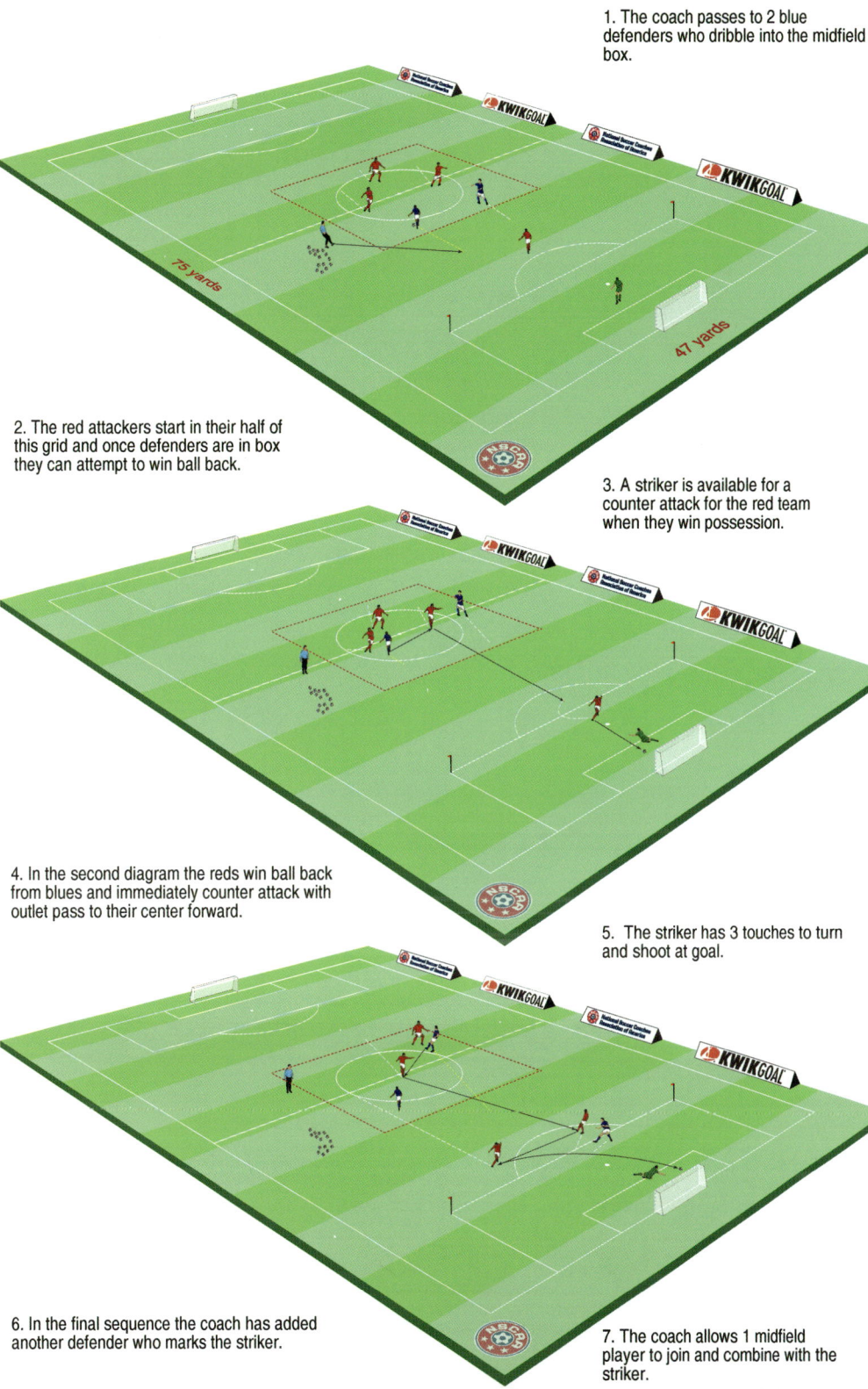

1. The coach passes to 2 blue defenders who dribble into the midfield box.

2. The red attackers start in their half of this grid and once defenders are in box they can attempt to win ball back.

3. A striker is available for a counter attack for the red team when they win possession.

4. In the second diagram the reds win ball back from blues and immediately counter attack with outlet pass to their center forward.

5. The striker has 3 touches to turn and shoot at goal.

6. In the final sequence the coach has added another defender who marks the striker.

7. The coach allows 1 midfield player to join and combine with the striker.

Why use it?

This activity replicates a game related defensive scenario focusing on the midfield and forward players. The objective is for the midfield players to win the ball back from the opposition and counter attack quickly by combining with the striker.

Set up

The activity is played on a 9v9 field with a 20x20 yards box straddling both sides of the half way line. The coach works with the team attacking the large goal. 3 midfield players and 1 striker start the game against 2 defenders and a goalkeeper. The 3 midfield players must start the activity in their half of the field. The coach stands adjacent to the box and has a large supply of balls.

How to play

The coach starts the activity with a pass to the 2 defenders starting outside the area. On receipt of the ball the 2 defenders enter the area and attempt to penetrate over the end line on the dribble. The 3 attackers try to deny penetration and win possession. Immediately, the player who wins the ball must attempt to pass to the striker who has 3 touches to score goal. Play 4 x 3 minute games. After a couple of rounds add a central defender and allow 1 midfielder to burst out of grid to support the striker to create a 2v1 to goal.

Coaching notes

Coaching Objectives: The midfield players should apply high pressure with a numerical advantage and collapse around the 2 defenders. After the ball is won, the attackers should transition to a counter attack and play forward quickly.
Coaching Tips: Adding a time or touch restriction for the attacking team increases the speed and intensity of the game. Game conditions require the team to play with urgency before the opponent is able to regroup and compact.

How to modify

Less Challenging: Start with 1 defender and move the box closer to the goal.
More Challenging: Add additional defenders, increase the size of the field and add time limits for the attacking team.

Stage/s of development covered by activity

Stages 4 & 5 - 12-18 year old players.

Development themes and competencies

Top 3 Themes: Defending as a unit, counter attacking and shooting.
Top 3 Competencies: Pressure and cover defending, tackling technique and communication.

DEFENDING 8v8 PLUS 1

Why use it?
This activity places players in a game related environment emphasizing the coordination of the team's defensive organization.

Set up
Play on a 9v9 field with two cone lines marked the width of the penalty box to narrow the field. The area is split into 3 equal size zones. Each team has 7 field players and a goalkeeper. The team in possession has an all-time offensive player to create a numerical advantage. Both teams set up in a 1-3-2-2 formation. The coach stands on the sideline to observe.

How to play
The defensive team works together in 3 defined lines (defense, midfield and forwards) in an attempt to make play predictable and win possession. The coach should help the players to identify visual cues and implement individual and small group defending strategies. The coach has a whistle and referees game. The coach should first observe and work on the relationship between 2 of the 3 lines, for instance the relationship between attacking line and the midfield line. Then progress to working with 3 lines and the players roles.

Coaching notes
Coaching Objectives: The defending team must organize the units/lines to make play predictable. The team should press forward and prevent progression towards the goal. Recovery runs can be addressed when ball gets behind a 'line'.
Coaching Tips: To place a defending team in moment of crisis, a player shooting at goal must run around a corner flag before recovering to help win the ball back.

How to modify
Less Challenging: Remove the all-time offensive player.
More Challenging: Widen the field and maintain a numerical advantage for the attacking team.

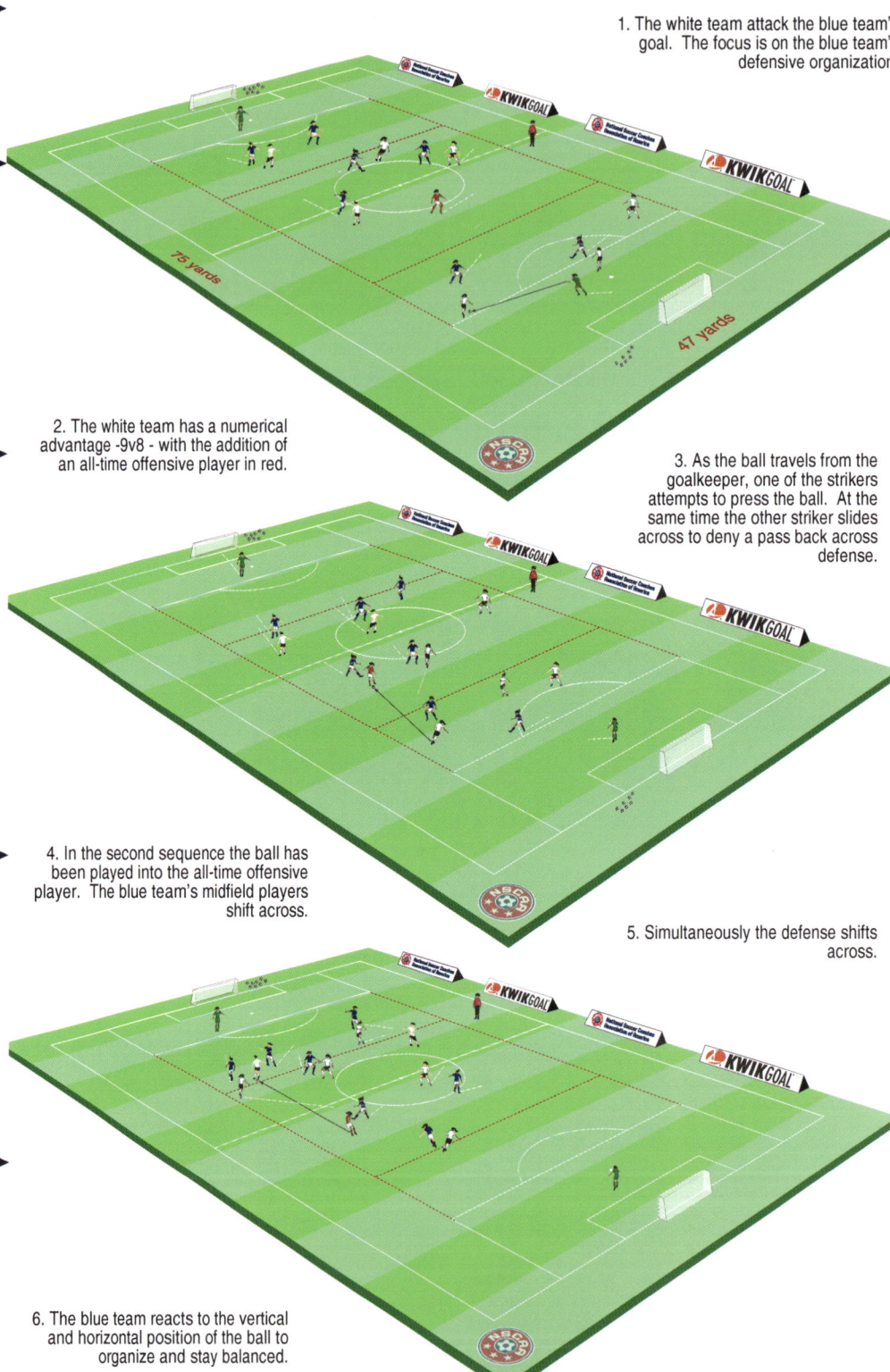

1. The white team attack the blue team's goal. The focus is on the blue team's defensive organization.

2. The white team has a numerical advantage -9v8 - with the addition of an all-time offensive player in red.

3. As the ball travels from the goalkeeper, one of the strikers attempts to press the ball. At the same time the other striker slides across to deny a pass back across defense.

4. In the second sequence the ball has been played into the all-time offensive player. The blue team's midfield players shift across.

5. Simultaneously the defense shifts across.

6. The blue team reacts to the vertical and horizontal position of the ball to organize and stay balanced.

Stage/s of development covered by activity
Stages 4 & 5 - 12-18 year old players.

Development themes and competencies

Top 3 Themes: Defending as a unit, counter attacking and shooting.

Top 3 Competencies: Pressure and cover defending, tackling technique and communication.

9v9 LOW PRESSURE DEFENDING

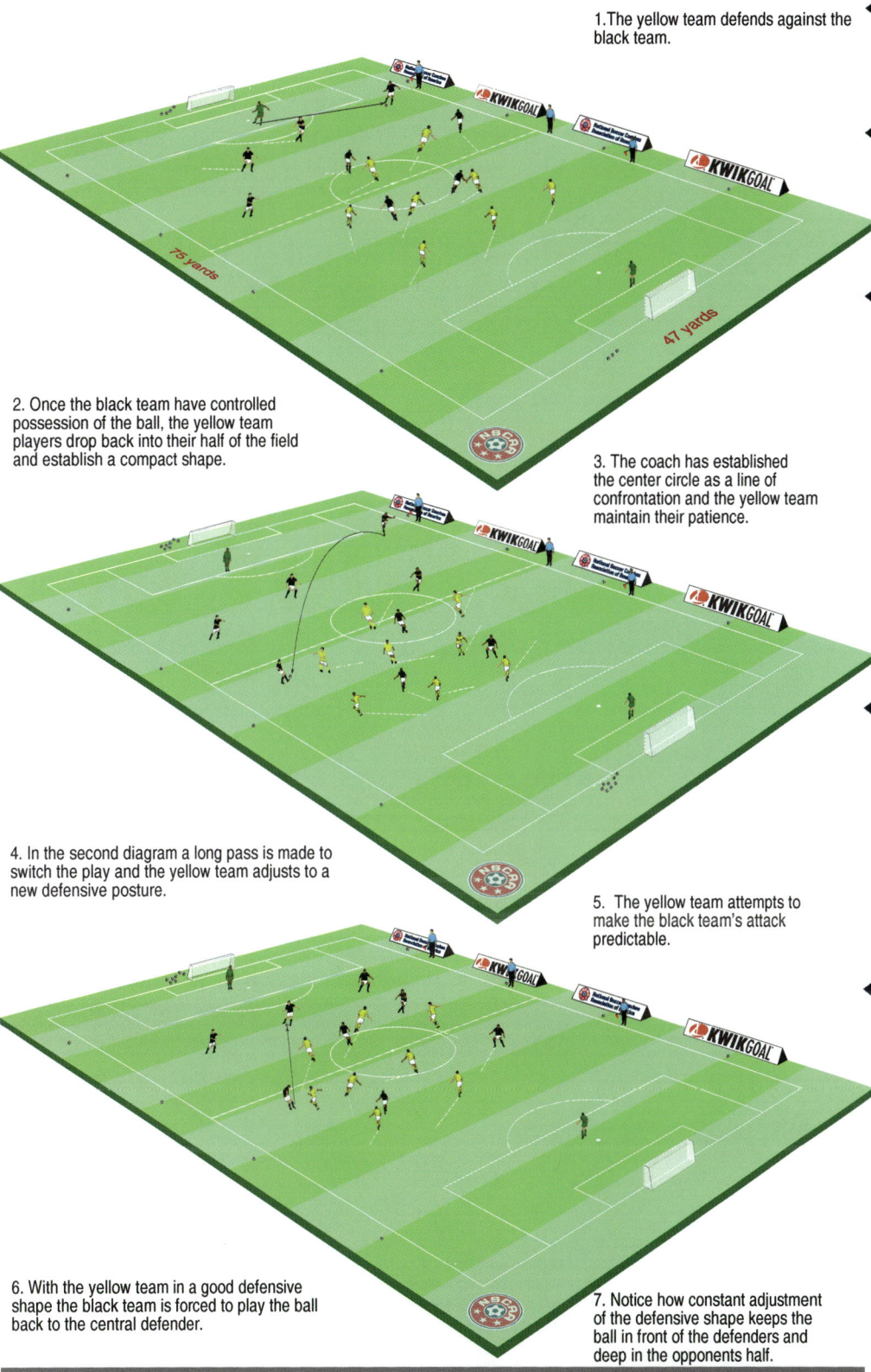

1. The yellow team defends against the black team.

2. Once the black team have controlled possession of the ball, the yellow team players drop back into their half of the field and establish a compact shape.

3. The coach has established the center circle as a line of confrontation and the yellow team maintain their patience.

4. In the second diagram a long pass is made to switch the play and the yellow team adjusts to a new defensive posture.

5. The yellow team attempts to make the black team's attack predictable.

6. With the yellow team in a good defensive shape the black team is forced to play the ball back to the central defender.

7. Notice how constant adjustment of the defensive shape keeps the ball in front of the defenders and deep in the opponents half.

Why use it?
This is an ideal activity for a team that is susceptible to counter attacks and is too slow to organize in defense.

Set up
2 teams play 9v9 field on a full field. Balls are placed around the field just off the sideline. The coach stands on the sideline to observe and instruct.

How to play
Play a regular game with both teams set up in a 1-3-3-2 formation. Make sure that balls are placed around the field at various points to get the game restarted quickly. Introduce situational play where the team you are coaching is winning 1-0 and must maintain a 1 goal lead for 5 minutes. The defensive objective is to recover the defensive shape with a low pressure approach. All players should drop back into the defensive half of the field and form a compact shape. This tactic will allow the attacking team time and space in front of the defense, leaving less room for the opponents to play through or over.

Coaching notes
Coaching Objectives: Work with players and their angles and speed of recovery. The first instinct must be to get back between your goal and the ball and then once the defense is organized start to exert pressure.
Coaching Tips: Communication between the defenders is crucial to coordinate the movement of the defensive unit.

How to modify
Less Challenging: Reduce the number of attackers and decrease the size of the playing area.
More Challenging: Add a touch restriction or time target for the attacking team to speed up play.

Stage/s of development covered by activity
Stages 4 & 5 - 12-18 year old players.

Development themes and competencies
Top 3 Themes: Defending as a unit, low pressure and shooting.
Top 3 Competencies: Recovery runs, defensive shape of the team and communication.

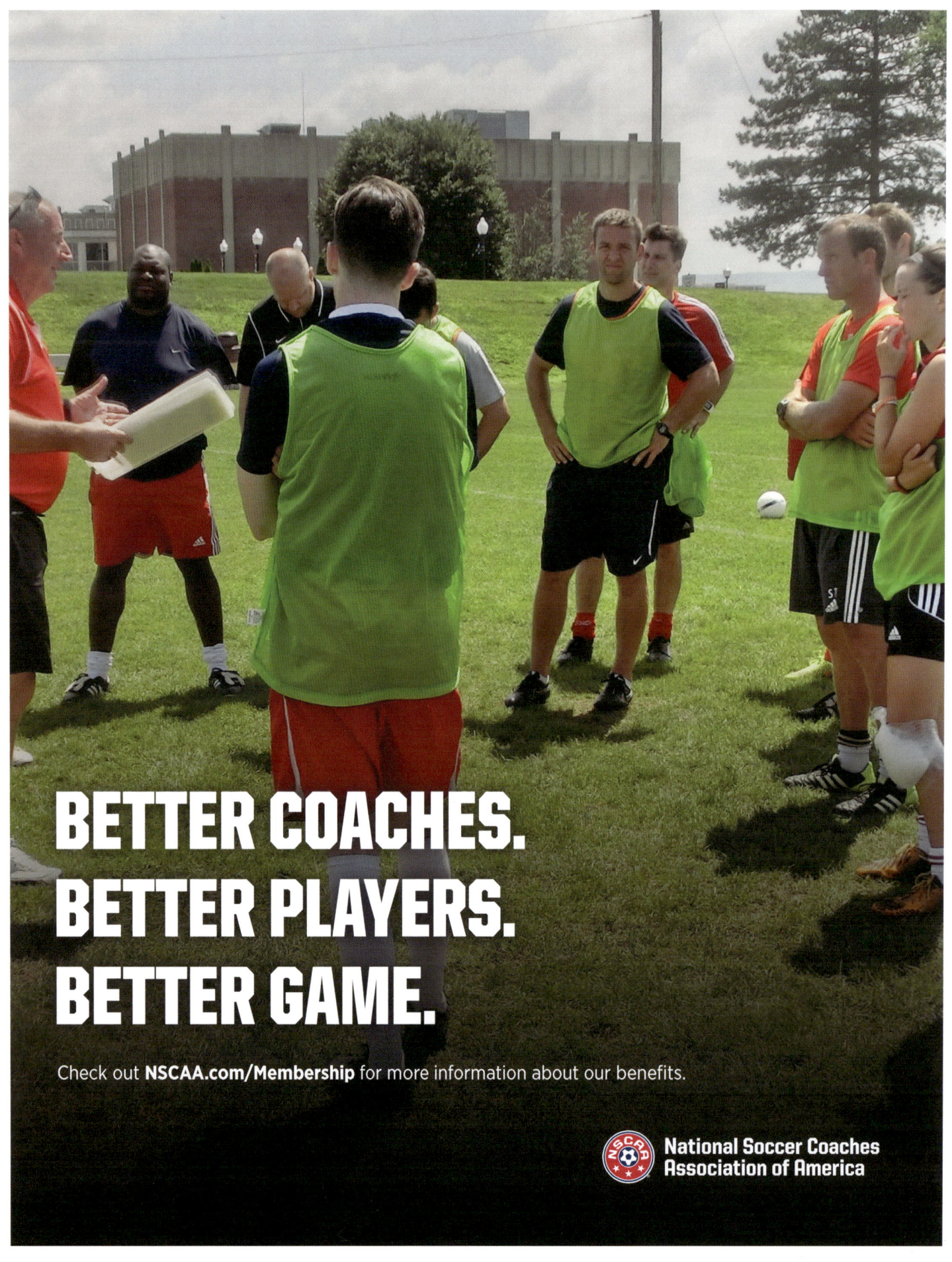